HOW TO PROMOTE YOUR OWN BUSINESS

This book is dedicated to my
daughters Susannah and Sarah

HOW TO PROMOTE YOUR OWN BUSINESS

A Guide to Low Budget Publicity

Jim Dudley

KOGAN PAGE

Acknowledgements

I would like to thank those people and firms who helped me prepare *How to Promote Your Own Business*. First, Karen Towlson and Andrea Frame, valued colleagues who helped me put the manuscript together, Dorne Wright from DEW Marketing, John Wright from Publicity Profile Ltd, Rupert Pyrah from Ray Morgan and Partners and Clive Atkinson from Advanti Advertising and Marketing Ltd, who advised me on the media planning and advertising chapters, as well as Norman Hart from Interact Communications Ltd, who allowed me to use his material in the first chapter. I would also like to thank the following companies and organisations: The Boots Company plc, The National Westminster Bank plc, *Marketing Week* and *The Director*.

Copyright © Jim Dudley 1988

All rights reserved

First published in Great Britain in 1988
by Kogan Page Limited,
120 Pentonville Road, London N1 9JN

British Library Cataloguing in Publication Data
Dudley, Jim
  How to promote your own business: a
  guide to low budget publicity.
  1. Publicity
  I. Title
  659.2   HM263

  ISBN 1-85091-524-5
  ISBN 1-85091-230-0 Pbk

Printed and bound in Great Britain by
Biddles Limited, Guildford

Contents

Acknowledgements   iv

Introduction   vii

1. *Promoting Your Own Business*   1

Promotional tools 1; Ingredients for a successful business 2; Defining your business 3; The keys to successful promotion 5; Packaging your image 9

2. *Advertising*   12

Types of advertising 13; Adoption stages 14; Influence on the market of early users 15; Rules for effective advertising 16; Cost of advertising 20; Codes of practice and influencing bodies 20

3. *Public Relations*   23

Targeting news 25; Cost-effectiveness 26; What constitutes PR activity 26; Evaluating PR 27

4. *Sales Promotion, Merchandising, Selling and Exhibiting*   28

Sales promotion activities 28; Types of sales promotion 29; In-store merchandising 34; Selling 38; Telemarketing 39; Exhibitions 41

5. *Designing Press Advertisements*   45

Develop a creative strategy 46; Find a unique feature of your product or service 46; Position your product 48; Target audience 48; Creative execution of the strategy 49; Writing the copy 50; Selecting a designer 55; Briefing the designer and checking artwork 56; Other types of press advertisement 59

6. *Designing Posters and Leaflets*   62

Posters 62; Leaflets 66; Direct mail — letters 73

7. *Direct Response Advertising* — 77

Success requirements 77; Principles of direct response marketing 78; Direct response marketing sequences 78; Catalogues 79; Integration into the sales attack 85; Mail order schemes for protecting the consumer buying through cash-off-the-page advertisements 88; Royal Mail services 94

8. *Making News* — 95

News stories 95; Press receptions 98; Gaining countrywide publicity 100; How to generate national publicity 101; Appearing on TV 104; Radio interviews 107; Personal photograph 107

9. *News Release Service* — 108

Writing a news release 108; Presentation and despatching 115; Use of photographs 119; Reporters 121; Photographers 122

10. *Financial Planning of Promotional Activity* — 124

Look at the big picture 124; Methods of allocating money to promotion 125; Payback calculations 126; Setting budgets 127; Cut-off points 129

11. *Media Planning* — 130

Mainstream media 130; Television 130; Press 133; Radio 139; Cinema 139; Posters 140; Direct mail 141; Media for the local business 141; Making a media plan 144; Weight of advertising 147; Determining the weight of the campaign 148; Media schedule 156

12. *Selecting an Advertising Agency* — 157

The selection process 158; Paying the agency 161

13. *Choosing a PR Consultancy* — 162

14. *Planning your Promotional Activities* — 165

Put the plan down on paper 166; Five stages to mounting the promotional programme 167; Further tips on running your own business 171

Appendices — 173

Index — 187

Introduction

The aim of this book is to help you to promote your own business. The text is designed to prepare you to use a set of promotional tools to improve your sales, win the confidence of backers and sources of finance, and to gain help from your suppliers and everyone else from whom you will need support to make your business grow and prosper.

The ideas contained in this book are not just to do with the technical aspects of publicity management nor the jargon of the professional. They are to do with using promotional tools and techniques to create a dialogue with your market and other interested groups within society. The book aims both to help and motivate you to get out there and start promoting your business for more growth and more profits.

The book concentrates on your needs and strives to show you:

- how to focus on what you want to achieve to make your business prosper;
- how to use promotional tools professionally;
- how to create exciting and effective campaigns at low cost;
- how to get publicity for nothing;
- how to plan your promotional costs and investment;
- how to choose and use professional advisers;
- how to improve your skills and capabilities;
- how to run your own business effectively.

This book is different from others on publicity management or marketing for four basic reasons:

- It focuses on the total promotional requirements of the small business: not only sales promotion but promotion of the organisation as a whole.

Introduction

- It covers the whole spectrum of promotional activity, ie communication, advertising, public relations, sales promotion, exhibiting, selling, direct response marketing, merchandising and customer service.
- It not only shows you how to get things done; it provides references and check lists to help you get started.
- *How to Promote Your Own Business* is written in everyday language.

Most texts on the subject of promotion or publicity-related topics ignore people who need a broadly based guide. The professional or academic will often specialise in one specific field and as a result it is difficult for the reader to view the 'big picture' of promotional options.

How to Promote Your Own Business tries to cover every important aspect of promotion to give you sufficient knowledge either to try your hand on a 'do it yourself' basis or to use professional support. Included in the text are many tips and ideas already tested and of proven success.

CHAPTER 1
Promoting Your Own Business

Most people running businesses today are aware of a need to create publicity for their products and firms. This book is about using marketing communication techniques to help you develop and enlarge your business. By being good at promoting your business you will be able to influence people's attitudes and opinions in its favour and in favour of the products or services you are selling. Through good communication you will be able to get your ideas across to customers, financial backers, suppliers, employees and everyone else in the community upon whose goodwill your growth and survival depend.

Promoting your business means using comunication skills and finding the right promotional tools to create a dialogue with your market. In the pages which follow we will describe those promotional tools which we feel are most relevant and useful to the small business.

The promotional tools described in this book can be adapted for use in all businesses, big or small, but we will concentrate on those aspects of promotion that you will be able to manage yourself. You will, we hope, be quite surprised at the successes you can achieve by promoting your own business effectively, using your own talents.

Promotional tools

For the purposes of description we have divided the principal promotional tools into four basic spheres of activity, namely:

Advertising
Sales promotion
Selling
Public Relations

These four basic areas are the promotional tools around which this text is based. If you can understand the role that each plays in promoting a business and then orchestrate them into an overall campaign, you will enjoy considerable success. In evolving a promotional plan you will need to set up strategies for each of the four promotional tools by taking into account the various aspects and characteristics of each. You should then develop the four tools into comprehensive campaign.

By the end of this book you will see that there are a number of options that you select in putting together a 'mix' of activity, yet the key to successful promotion is to get as much of your activity working together as you can and be persistent in seeking opportunities to create promotional activity which focuses attention on your firm and the products which you are selling.

Ingredients for a Successful Business

The fundamental aim of promoting your business is to create a dialogue with your market and those institutions which will help it thrive and grow. This aim must, however, support an organisation which has all the necessary ingredients to be successful.

A successful business is therefore one which knows where it is going, has competitive products or services to offer its customers, and is fully supported by good customer service.

At the same time it must have enough resources to finance its stock, facilities and people so that the business is run properly. Any business which fails in any of these features is going to be very vulnerable.

From studies carried out it would seem that the most important aspects of a company's image and reputation are:

- Product performance (or in the case of a service company the services it offers)
- The organisation's ability to deliver on time
- The quality of the organisation's advertising and sales promotional material.

It is how an organisation's 'offerings' stack up in terms of performance, services and the way these are presented promotionally which will decide whether it flourishes or flounders in today's competitive markets.

If your products fail to perform or your service falls short of customer expectations then your business will soon lose credibility. A lack of credibility among customers will soon spill over to affect the way your backers, bankers, suppliers and employees perceive your operation.

In promoting your business, then, you should ensure that your image and reputation are built around *your product or service performance* and the way you present it. No matter how much gloss you put on your business it must always be supported by the assurance that what you are selling meets your customers' expectations and is maintained by good customer service support. You must be able to offer satisfaction through your product and be able to present it in such a way that will be believable.

Figure 1.1 has been developed by Interact Seminars in a special study of corporate relations. It is useful in two respects. First you can use it as a checklist around which to build your corporate image and reputation and second you can use it for its main purpose, which is to enable you to rate your own image.

Defining your business

Many small businesses have become extremely successful when they have established a good base of regular customers and no longer run on a series of ad hoc deals. There are advantages to be gained if you can plan the general direction in which you want to go. For example you can:

- Plan your resources and investments to match demand from customers
- Develop skills from within your organisation to provide and develop competitive products
- Provide good customer service support
- Build up a solidly based company image in the eyes of your customers.

The idea of defining its purpose is becoming increasingly popular in the small business. The principle is based on the answer to the questions 'What business are we in?' and 'What business do our customers think we are in?'

Let us take the example of three independent firms of insurance brokers who set out to sell insurance and life assurance in different ways.

The rating number is the maximum you can score against an item if you are very pleased with the impression it creates. If less pleased, reduce your score accordingly down to zero.

Message source	Rating	Score
Company name	5	
Letterheading	6	
Head office building	2	
Reception area	4	
Sales literature	7	
House style/logo/trade mark	5	
Switchboard response	6	
Price-list	2	
Company cars	2	
Notice boards	2	
Entertaining guests	3	
Product performance	8	
Product range	5	
Product appearance and packaging	4	
Distribution and agents	3	
Outside opinion, eg trade associations, competitors	4	
Chief executive speaking in public	5	
Salesmen	6	
Sales service	6	
Delivery times	7	
Applicants for jobs	2	
Advertising	7	
Press releases	4	
Exhibitions, displays, receptions	5	
Visual aids, films, photographs	1	
Business gifts	2	
Direct mail and letters	3	
Charity support	1	
Entries in directories	1	
Invoices, delivery notes, documentation	1	
Total	120	

How to assess your score.

If your score is above 100 then your image is really untarnished; well above average.

If you fall in the range 70 to 100 then your image is fair to good.

Below 70 calls for some action, and already from your score sheet you know which particular elements need attention.

There will be some assessments which are lower than 50. To those people there are two observations. One is that you are obviously remarkably honest. The other is that you could probably do with some professional help.

Reprinted with permission from the *Director*, December 1986.

Figure 1.1 *Assessing your image*

The first sets up a small community-based business offering a wide range of services. The second decides to specialise in pension planning for firms in a wider geographical area, and the third decides to specialise in vehcile fleet insurance for businesses.

Each firm could say, 'We are in the insurance business', but as each firm builds its reputation in the longer term:

- The first company is seen by its customers as a local insurance business from which advice, insurance, help with claims and a whole basket of 'add-on' services can be obtained. As this business evolves people will come to enquire about services and regular customers will come back to renew policies and seek new ones.
- The second company will be seen by its customers as pension planners from whom advice, recommendations, pension administration and other services can be acquired. This company can constantly add to its range of services through innovative schemes, initiating responses to market needs and adapting to changes in government regulations.
- The third company will be seen by its customers as experts in vehicle insurance. The business could evolve through helping fleet managers to get the best deals, advising on types of vehicles to buy and so on.

Each of these brokers' images will evolve from what each practice does best. Through promoting their products and their excellence in their respective fields each will build its reputation over the longer term. What should, however, be avoided is a situation where a strategy is adopted which attempts to make the same broker a pension planner on Monday and a vehicle fleet insurer on Friday – this will only confuse potential customers. It is through a sustained and consistent development of an image that a business creates a reputation which customers recognise and trust.

The keys to successful promotion

Successful promotion is designed to build a consistent image for the business among its customers and other special interest groups.

To be successful you need to:

- know your market
- know your target audiences
- maintain a sustained promotional programme.

Your market. The word market in the context of this book describes the potential demand for the products or services you have to sell. Every market is based on customers seeking the satisfaction of a need from competing suppliers. Markets involve customers, suppliers, distribution systems, communications and more often than not, regulatory systems. Every business operates within a market where customers seek to buy products and where suppliers try to tempt customers to buy their products. The important characteristic of almost all markets is that the customers have a choice and that suppliers have to compete to sell their products.

Many existing firms, through experience, research and acquired knowledge, tend to have a good idea of their market; the importance of this cannot be too highly stressed. You need to know how big your market is, your competitors, the customers, the distribution systems etc if you are to operate successfully within it. From the promotional point of view this information is essential in deciding how, where and when to direct your communication.

Here is a simple checklist which might be adapted to your business, around which you can compile data about your market.

- The industry
- The relevant sector
- The value of the sector
- Geographical catchment area
- Customer knowledge
- The ways or channels through which products or services reach the end user
- Principal competitors and vendors of substitute products
- Legal constraints under which the market operates
- Industry peculiarities and special customs
- Usual methods of advertising, selling and other promotional activity in the industry.

This data will be useful both in compiling a business plan which defines your business and in the development of your promotional activity. Obviously you have to find an area within your market that gives you enough scope and potential to develop your business.

Here you should apply the idea of defining your business by selecting a segment of the business you are in that will allow you to build a longer-term image and reputation.

Your target audiences. Your target audiences are those groups to whom you direct your promotional activity. The more precisely you can identify and aim your communications the more effective your promotional activity will be. The following groups are potential audiences.

Customers or potential customers are your most important audience. It is through recruiting customers that you will obtain the revenue necessary to run your business. This audience can be identified in three ways.

1. From knowledge of who your past and present customers are. Past customers are often more likely to buy from you than new ones. If your sort of business lends itself to maintenance of customer records, keep track of your past customers as they are your primary target.
2. There is every likelihood that other people who have similar characteristics to your past customers, eg sex, age, income, profession, special interests or locality will have the same needs as your existing customers. They therefore make a target as potential customers.
3. Your competitor's customers. Find out who they are and what particular likes or dislikes they have with regard to your competitor's products.

If you can do some market research to find out more about your customer audience then you start off from a better position of knowledge.

However, many small businesses have relatively easily identifiable customers, obviating the need for expensive research in this area. Others build up a good 'feel' for their customers by keeping good records.

Distribution channels and intermediaries are commonly referred to as the 'trade'. Trade audiences are quite easily identifiable in most industry categories. Buyers, sellers, agents or whatever they are called in your industry are important, in that their decision to stock your product or promote your service may influence your ability to get your products into your customer's hands. These audiences can be identified through the following:

1. Your own knowledge and trade records. Your existing customers are most likely to be those from whom you can expect the most support. They will obviously be your primary target.
2. Use trade directories such as Kelly's (available in your library) to produce lists of potential trade customers and reach these through techniques we will describe later.
3. Collect names from enquiries, collect business cards, keep

registers at exhibitions, read and research the trade press. The bigger your database the more contacts you have to work on.

The next group of audiences is one from which support and influence can be exploited for the furtherance of your cause. For example:

Journalists and opinion formers are people you can use to form a communications bridge with your market. We have devoted Chapters 3, 8 and 9 to ways of making the media and opinion formers work for you.

Backers, investors, financial institutions, banks etc are your sources of finance and will need to be convinced of your viability and potential. You will need to identify these special interest groups and seek to communicate with them. This particular target is very impressed by company performance and by the potential for any innovation you want to introduce. Aim communications at this group, inform them of your business success, your innovations and your professional approach.

The Local community in general is an important target. Your aim is to win community support.

Employees and staff are also a very important target. The larger you get the harder it will be to communicate with your own people. The target is easily identifiable but do not forget most people have families and so include them in your target.

Suppliers are an often ignored target audience. Yet very often the small business is at the mercy of major suppliers through their policies for 'credit', price discounts and service. Your financial credibility and importance as a customer will need to be emphasised. Call on them to help you with promotion and sales support – you both make money that way.

Maintain a sustained and consistent promotional programme. The two words which should be emphasised are *sustained* and *consistent*.

Promotion is not something you do just once. It is a business activity which must be sustained. You must also be equally determined to ensure that everything that is done to achieve an image for your products and organisation is *consistent*. You cannot be one thing one day and something else the next. A loaf of bread which is promoted one week as a wholesome nutritious family food cannot be promoted the next as a slimming aid without creating confusion in the customer's mind. Too many businesses come unstuck by chopping and changing what they are saying about their products and themselves.

Packaging your image

Focus your promotional activities through what you do or the product you sell rather than who you are. The name of your product or service is more important than your company name in nearly all cases. Let your product or service build up your image and reputation. Every time you bring out a calendar or give away a pen let it bear your product name; you can always add your company name but prominence should be devoted to your product or service.

In the normal order of things anybody setting up in business usually starts with designing letterheadings, business cards, developing a logo style and so forth. Thus it would seem that this would be a useful place for us to start.

Your stationery, business cards, van livery and so forth are very often the first things which potential customers, suppliers, bank managers and others see when a new business is born.

Let's look at how you might approach developing what we might call your 'house style'. First your house style should convey some idea or tone which is relevant in reinforcing your business image.

Start off by getting your company name right. It should reflect what you want the market to think you are good at. The closer it is to describing your product or service, the more closely will your company and product be associated in your customers' minds.

Your house style in terms of print and graphics on your notepaper, etc should be compatible with the sort of business you are in.

A computer software company, for example, with the house style more compatible with that of a hairdresser may not be as convincing as one with a style more reflective of programming expertise. Brief a designer (even print shops have some reasonable designers) that your image and house style need to reflect the business you are in and convey some aspect of it you believe sets you apart from other contestants in the market. Keep it clear and simple. It's not necessary to design some complicated logo style at the outset – you might be embarrassed by it later.

Decide on 'house colours'; use them as a theme on stationery, vehicle livery, shop frontages, reception areas, company ties, etc. Don't forget that colour styles change; what might be in this year may be yuk the next.

Having designed your overall theme in terms of house style,

graphics and colour, your next step is to make sure that everything you print, paint or paper over is dedicated to:

- communicating who you are and what you are selling
- providing every opportunity to let people useful to your business know how to contact you
- reinforcing your indentity and providing the basis around which you can build a product or service and company image.

Everything which carries your house style, advertises your products, carries your goods to market should project your business. Everything should also have your phone number on it!

Your house style and livery are not your corporate image. It is the packaging of your image around what you are good at and what satisfies your customers when they deal with you.

Brand names

The brand name identifies the product for a buyer and gives the supplier the opportunity to create a reliable franchise of repeat users. A brand is a name, term, sign or symbol, or a combination of them, which is intended to identify the goods and services of one seller or group of sellers and to differentiate them from competitors.

The use of a brand name enables the marketing company to encapsulate all the product's physical and psychological benefits into a single entity. In other words it gives the total product concept a name that consumers can recognise and ask for.

Logos and trade marks also add credibility to products. Boots, ICI, Weetabix, Bovril and Rolls-Royce logos confirm to consumers that the products originate from firms with a high reputation. Brand names should be registered: this is an important factor which should not be overlooked if the company's rights are to be protected.

Reinforcing your image

Customer service is a major promotional tool. It is one of the foundations of business success. Always remember that customer satisfaction *begins after* you have made the sale. Customer satisfaction should be nurtured, because as long as your customers enjoy what you have sold them your reputation will hold good with them.

Past customers are very often your best and most loyal. Not only are they the most likely to buy again from you but they will also sing your praises. Badly treated customers not only avoid buying from you but also become your adversaries in the market-place. Ensure therefore that you place high on your priorities the need to ensure longer-term customer satisfaction.

The more customers you recruit the harder it will be to maintain a high level of customer service. We have stressed this idea throughout the book to remind you that good service is the best way to generate promotion and publicity at minimal cost. Getting your customers to promote your business for you is very cheap and you won't be paying an advertising agency commission on it.

CHAPTER 2
Advertising

Given sufficient funds the advertiser can aim at and hit a target of readers, viewers or listeners many times.

Advertising in its role as a persuasive method of communication can be used in two different ways:

- direct response
- indirect response.

Direct response advertising involves asking the potential customer to respond by buying direct from the advertiser. An example is a life assurance advertisement, which asks readers to fill in a reply coupon for information on the policies offered. The impact of the advertising on the receiver is to persuade that person to respond directly.

Indirect response advertising involves persuading an audience to find and purchase a product or service from an intermediary. Demand is created by continuously exposing an audience to an advertising message. It is important, however, to ensure that products are easily obtainable. For indirect advertising to work effectively, distribution and merchandising play a vital role in the organisation's activities.

Advertising then is used as an economical way of speaking to a great number of people with similar needs in order to inform and persuade them to take a particular course of action, whether it be to sell them a Rolls-Royce or to get them to ring a double glazing representative.

Alas, very many people have a number of misconceptions about advertising which adversely affect their ability to use it professionally, for example:

Advertising can make anybody buy anything.
Advertising uses psychological techniques which deprive the average person of his ability to make rational judgements about what is advertised.
People use advertising dishonestly to cheat the public.
Advertising is composed of novelties or gimmicks to make it work.
Advertising makes a poor product appear better than it is.

These common misconceptions unfortunately have the effect of perpetuating examples of malpractice if only because non-professional advertisers believe these misconceptions to the point that they try to use advertising in a dishonest way. *Dishonest advertising will quickly ruin any cause or business.*

Let us therefore attempt to dispel these misconceptions from the outset.

Types of advertising

There are basically three types of advertising, namely:
- *Consumer advertising* is advertising aimed at the ordinary consumer and is typified by what is seen on TV, heard on the radio or read in newspapers, magazines and so forth. This is mass communication aimed at large numbers of potential purchasers in an effort to pre-sell the advertiser's products to them and create demand from targeted consumers.
- *Trade advertising,* ie advertising aimed at wholesalers, retailers, brokers, agents and those who are part of an advertiser's distribution system. Wholesalers buy from the advertiser, retailers buy from the wholesaler and sell to the consumer. The purpose of trade advertising is to persuade wholesalers and retailers to stock the advertiser's products, which in turn makes it easier for the consumer to find and purchase the advertiser's product.
- *Business to users advertising*, ie advertising directed at industrial consumers. Here, advertisers' products are bought by industrial customers, who use them as suppliers of services, eg raw materials, or as consumers, eg buyers of disposable hats.

The basic principles of advertising are common to each type of advertising, apart from the fact that orientation and media selection will tend to be more specialised for the second and third types of advertising.

Adoption stages

There are five stages through which a potential consumer passes before adopting a new product. We might call these *acceptance stages*, as follows:

1. *Awareness*. The potential customer gets to know the product but lacks information about it.
2. *Interest*. The potential customer is stimulated to seek information about the product.
3. *Evaluation*. The potential customer considers whether it would make sense to try the product.
4. *Trial*. The individual tries the product on a small scale, by taking a sample or testing the product.
5. *Adoption*. The individual decides to make full and regular use of the product.

These five stages are a learning process through which the potential customer will pass in the process of becoming a *regular user*.

Each individual is likely to go through the process at a different rate and many will not become regular users. The factors affecting the speed of an adoption process by a large number of individuals (who make up the product market) will depend upon how long it takes for individuals to become aware of the product idea and their propensity to try it. There is an inter-relationship between the individual's adoption stages and the diffusion process. People vary in their willingness to try new products, some are prepared to try them as soon as they become available, others are more conservative. For example, many business people acquired personal computers (PCs) when they were first introduced to help them run their businesses, others awaited evidence that the PC could be a useful tool. Many more will not acquire a PC for many years to come.

Influence on the market of early users

Some early adopters, if they are entirely satisfied with the product or service they are using, will encourage other people to try it. This role of early adopters influencing the market has been empirically proved, and is very important because:

- positive comments from these people will greatly speed up the

diffusion of the product idea throughout the market;
- on the other hand, negative comments from early users could well have the effect of slowing down general acceptance of the product.

In planning a new introduction to the market, therefore, the need to ensure that the product lives up to expectations is paramount, but you must also ensure that:
- your advertising creates the sort of expectations in the consumer's mind that are best met by the product's principal benefits so that they buy for the right reasons
- you constantly reinforce customer attitudes to your products long after they have started buying them. You will improve customer relations by remembering that customer satisfaction begins with the purchase of your product
- you ensure that by good customer service you reinforce your own company image and hold on to existing customers.

Remember, then, that satisfied users of your products will have a large influence on the general acceptance of your product by the market as a whole.

However, for advertising to be effective in recruiting customers two conditions need to be met: potential customers must first, have a need for what is offered (whether it is perceived or not), and second, be able to take up what is offered (that is, they have sufficient money, they are the right age, sex or have the physical ability).

Thus someone selling wheelchairs is not going to be able to persuade people in perfect health to rush along and buy one for themselves nor will the advertiser of VIP jets increase his orders from those of us with average earnings.

You might now be asking yourself whether advertising can be economical if many people cannot take up the offers because they have neither the need nor the ability. Yet it is; because mingled among thousands of such people there are likely to be some who have both the need and the ability, and effective advertising will persuade them to take up the offer, and what's more, introduce your offer to their friends. To reach these people in any other way would be too costly both in terms of physical resources and money.

Unfortunately, because advertising tends to influence our way of life and because we are so frequently confronted with it on television, radio, in the papers and magazines we read, and even in the streets and shops, many people tend to view it with suspicion. To some extent this suspicion is justified when there is any obvious malpractice. By and large, however, both legal and voluntary controls on advertising have reduced such examples to the extent that they have become the exception rather than the rule.

Rules for effective advertising

Advertising contributes to the success of an organisation through the part it plays in initiating and sustaining the diffusion process through the recruitment of customers who sample and adopt the organisation's offerings. Successful advertising works by:

- attracting attention of the consumer
- creating interest
- stimulating trial
- stimulting continuous usage of the product among consumers
- continuing to convince users of the product that it is superior to competitors' products by reinforcing consumer attitudes.

Effective advertising is achieved through careful observance of the following rules.

- deliver a competitive and stimulating message
- target the message to the right people (targeted audience)
- advertise often enough for the message to have an impact on the target audience (campaign)
- mount campaigns at times when the target audience is in the mood to try the product and when they are able to try the product.

Deliver a competitive and stimulating message

A drab uninteresting advertisement will not attract attention as effectively as one which makes the most of the available space; one which is creative, interesting and has a convincing message.

The best message will inevitably be one which correctly interprets the consumer's need for the product or service and best emphasises its unique features. It is often difficult to persuade small business advertisers that consumers will very often perceive the products or service from the point of view of benefits offered.

For example, a life assurance policy to the consumer is security or a means of saving. To the insurance broker the assurance policy is seen as a variety of technical components: a policy with profits, without profits, equity based, unit trust linked, and so on. In addition the policy means a commission to the broker and maybe a new customer and always more paperwork. Remember to sell the benefits first and foremost not the product.

The key to a good and effective message is to ensure that the product advertised represents the consumer's perception and not the advertiser's and to ensure that the presentation is attractive. We will look at this important aspect of advertising in more detail in Chapter 5.

Target the message
We need then to produce a persuasive message which will appeal directly to people with the ability to take up the offer. The message naturally has to compete with other advertising and should amplify the principal benefits of the offer whilst attracting the attention of those people who are most likely to take up the offer. For example, if we were advertising to women we would ensure that our advertising was produced to appeal to women (see Chapter 5).

The people at whom we aim our advertising should, as far as possible, be broadly identified as a particular group within society (their propensity to respond to our advertising being their essential feature). We call this group our *target audience*.

In determining our target audience we could break it down into seven groups:

1. sex
2. age
3. size of family
4. income
5. special interests
6. life style
7. location

Obviously the better we can define the target audience the more accurately the message and the media can be selected.

For example, we might interest young women who like to cook, who have children, and who come from say low to middle income families. The target audience definition is quite simple in that it defines sex, age and family criteria.

But how do we express income? Well, sociologists have mapped out the British population using a sort of demographic shorthand – and this is worth knowing because you may need it in discussing your advertising with professionals.

Above-average income	A:	Upper class—high-income groups
	B:	Professional class.
Average income	C1:	White collar, working people.
	C2:	Blue collar, skilled working people.
Below-average income	D:	Unskilled, lower-paid working people.
	E:	The members of the community with very low income.

It is sometimes said that this class breakdown is a way of perpetuating class-consciousness – it is not intended to be so. It is meant as a convenient form of shorthand which enables the audience to be described. It is used because the question of income is one of the governing factors in deciding on the group of people with the highest propensity to act on the advertising message: have they the means to take up the offer? Of course, in some cases their income may also influence their need to take up the offer.

The important issue about this classification is that media owners often describe their audiences or readers in such terms. There is, however, a growing belief that, as British society increases its level of disposable income (and despite the unemployment figures, it is doing so) demographic classification is an incomplete method of defining audiences for many products or services.

Experience records. Keep details of customers or people making enquiries and see if a typical customer begins to emerge. In addition remember that past customers are most likely to be future customers, so keep names and addresses for future use – they are very valuable; do not lose them.

Desk research. This is a term coined by marketing and advertising people for digging out information about customers and markets. It basically means searching trade journals, government statistics, trade statistics and so on until enough information is gleaned to provide a profile of typical users – and this translates into a target audience.

Advertise often enough

Sufficient weight for advertising is essential in that the advertisement will have to compete for the reader's attention and action both with other advertisements and the reader's interests. (See Chapter 11.)

What has already been said about diffusion of the product idea should be taken into consideration here. Weight of advertising means frequency of exposure by audience or readers to an advertisement. Naturally, the newer the product and the more competitive the market, the greater the weight of advertising that will be required. The difference in advertisement requirements for a new brand of baked beans compared with the launching of a new computer software house, would be enormous. It would take several million pounds for the baked beans business to make an impact, whereas the computer software house could probably make an impact with a few thousand pounds properly targeted. The weight argument is concerned with the successful reach of the target audience and the number of times the message needs to be received by the target audience for there to be a response in terms of purchases.

Advertise at a time when people can take action
Timing is frequently one of the most overlooked aspects of advertising. Advertising needs to be given time to reach its audience and time for the audience to assimilate the message and respond. Very often, advertisers offering Christmas products start advertising in November or even October, to ensure that the maximum response comes in time for Christmas. Holiday travel firms start advertising after Christmas.

Advertising a seasonal sale, a theatrical performance or a promotional event needs careful consideration when it comes to timing. If it is too early people forget; if it is too late many people may not have time enough to alter their plans. One way of dealing with this problem is to advertise the event a week before, thus warning the public that the event is going to take place. Then place an advertisement on the day before, reminding the public to attend.

Continuous advertising to remind consumers of a product may not need precise timing except that there are often seasonal influences, many of which are not so obvious. Advertise when consumers are in the mood to act (cold treatments in winter) and when they are ready to act (ordering a summer holiday in January). Remember the key to good marketing is in the business of finding similarities between consumer need and producer offering. In advertising, where there is an investment risk, you need to find out how people behave and advertise to them accordingly. Here some form of research may be a good investment. A great number of attempts to change seasonality of product consumption have failed – so for the small budget advertiser play it safe and don't take more risks than are absolutely necessary. Using promotional tools is a skill and mistakes, whilst providing object lessons, are expensive.

Remember too that the best time to advertise is when people need you and it therefore stands to reason that advertising in Yellow Pages and *bona fide* trade directories can be an effective way of trawling for customers.

Cost of advertising

The costs of advertising really need to be compared with the costs of trying to achieve the organisation's objectives by other means. For example, using sales staff to canvass house by house may not be as effective as direct response advertising and using potential customer enquiries as leads for sales staff.

The economies of reaching relatively large numbers of potential customers through advertising commend it as a means of generating business. Often, when time, resources and costs of finding other means of communicating with customers are compared to advertising, advertising comes out on top.

Finding the funds to achieve weighting requirements is often a difficult problem for small advertisers. No matter what the calculations are on the returns expected from the advertising campaign, risks often outweigh the anticipated profits. If the bank manager says no, dreams of fame and fortune are dissipated immediately.

Here are a few ideas for finding the funds:

- First, narrow down the geography so that a small region can be reached effectively and then expand as funds become available.
- Piggy-back on national campaigns if you are in a group, franchise or national voluntary body. Or how about talking to suppliers, customers or even the media to do joint advertising? Can you get your product in someone else's catalogue?
- Combine advertising with free publicity techniques so that sufficient weight of communication may be created to ensure a customer response.

Codes of Practice and influencing bodies

The public is protected from unscrupulous advertising by a variety of legal and voluntary rules, and legal advice should be taken for each campaign. A Code of Practice has been set up to keep public confidence in advertising and is reinforced by the watchdog body, the Advertising Standards Authority.

Advertising Standards Authority
The ASA is an independent body established and financed by the British advertising business. It exists to protect the public from advertisers whose advertisements mislead, misrepresent, or offend. It has a responsibility for overseeing the implementation of the British Code of Advertising Practice and also the British Code of Sales Promotion Practice. The majority of the members of the Authority's Council and its Chairman must be entirely unconnected with advertising. Those members of the Council with experience of advertising sit as individuals and not as representatives of any sectional interest.

Code of Advertising Practice Committee
The CAP Committee is the central executive and policy-making organ of the advertising industry's system of self-regulation. Subject only to the general superintendence of the Advertising Standards Authority, whose function is to ensure the operation of the whole system in the public interest, the CAP Committee takes responsibility for seeing that the Code itself is kept up to date and that its member organisations work harmoniously together, with each playing its part in making sure that the Code is complied with. Anyone in the advertising industry, whether a member of the sponsoring organisation or not, may seek the Committee's advice, ask it to investigate a complaint or make recommendations to it as to how the Code or its own procedures might be improved.

The Advertising Association
The Advertising Association, founded in 1926, is a company listed by guarantee without a share capital and is a non-profit-making concern. More recently it has become more of a federation, as its primary member organisations are trade associations in the advertising, marketing and related fields. The main aims of the Association are as follows: to promote public confidence in advertising; to establish that responsible advertising is an essential factor in the marketing of goods and services, and in the economic life of the country; to demonstrate the efficiency of the service that advertising can give to government, industry and the public; to safeguard the common interests of those engaged in or using advertising by the promotion of common action and the support of protective measures; to persuade officials and legislators in this country, Europe and elsewhere to remove or modify regulatory provisions adverse to the interests of the advertising industry, and industry generally; to encourage a

continuing improvement in standards and efficiency of communication, of which advertising is a part.

Communication, Advertising and Marketing Education Foundation Ltd

CAM is the nationally recognised examining body for the communications industry. It was founded in 1969 by bringing together the educational bodies of the Advertising Association, the Institute of Practitioners in Advertising and the Institute of Public Relations. CAM is an educational charity set up to integrate a system of education and training in the related fields of communication, public relations, advertising and marketing, leading to the professional qualifications in the industry.

Association of Mail Order Publishers

An organisation founded with the aim of acquainting the general public and the media with the nature of its activities, the protection it offers to the consumer and the benefits of buying by post.

Mail order promotion techniques and the problems arising out of the customer/company relation have frequently been misunderstood, and have given rise to criticism in the past. The purpose of the Association is to correct misconceptions and to explain to the consumer his rights and privileges in the trading relation. It comprises leading publishers of books and audio products who trade directly with the consumer primarily by mail.

CHAPTER 3
Public Relations

Public Relations, or PR as it is more commonly designated, is an effective means of communication. The sales potential of good publicity means that many businesses have geared themselves to getting material printed or broadcast as virtually free advertising through making their companies and products newsworthy. It is true too that businesses that are seen to be successful very often are. Not only do they win and hold the respect of their customers, but also and as importantly, they enjoy the support of suppliers, employees, bankers and financial institutions as well as the local community.

Organisations successful in public relations are conscious of the way their businesses appear to the outside world. PR is used to help the organisation relate to its community, customers, employees and backers and to build and sustain goodwill through good times and bad.

Much of PR activity is involved with the media. The making and developing of contacts in publishing and the broadcast media is an essential job for the PR person, if news about the company and its products is to be successfully disseminated.

Yet the fact that PR uses the editorial columns of newspapers and magazines and non-advertising spots on TV and radio makes the messages it transmits extremely effective for the following reasons:

- News emanating from the organisation reaches the reader or listener as a media-originated report, adding to its credibility. It is not seen as advertising.
- Stories reach audiences who might otherwise avoid sales staff and advertisements.
- Stories and events about the company or its products can, like advertising, be dramatised.

An important feature of PR is that the space occupied by news about companies and products is rarely paid for, although the costs of creating the news may be quite expensive. On a modest level, however, PR offers a very cost-efficient means of getting an organisation noticed and remembered. Also, properly planned and executed, PR can both support and enhance other aspects of the organisation's promotional attack.

PR is defined by the Institute of Public Relations as:

> 'The deliberate and sustained effort to establish and maintain mutual understanding between an organisation and its publics.'

The need to do this is not obvious to everyone, but when we see how much effort we are putting into our publicity activities, we are unlikely to achieve our objectives if there is no mutual understanding between the organisation and the people it is trying to interest. It should be remembered that the organisation's public relations problems are usually more fundamental than their publicity problems.

Public relations is not just free publicity. It has an essential role not only in supporting promotional activities, but by its effective implementation makes other promotional activity more effective and by establishing an understanding with the community as a whole, PR helps the business to thrive in other ways.

For the small business, relationships with the public are not just created by media but by the attitude of the entrepreneur and staff to the public as a whole. No matter how good a PR campaign is used, indifferent or surly staff can lose goodwill very quickly. People who have been offended by the organisation are likely to talk badly about it and this can only work to the detriment of the business.

Total PR is a concept which suggests that public relations is practised and projected at all levels of the business – from the head, the entrepreneur, to the delivery driver or service engineer. Total PR is about showing the world that you are successful, you will continue to be successful, and this is what you are doing to ensure your company and products will always be successful: good customer service backing good products about which you are constantly telling the world.

The diffusion effect, outlined in Chapter 2, applies as much here as it does to the section on advertising. Promote a good product and back it with total PR and the goodwill will reach all potential customers and supporters of the business. Belief in the theory of positive and negative diffusion brings home to the entrepreneur just how vulnerable success can be. If the market remains dispersed there is no take-off of sales – if it is disappointed with the company's offering, sales will come to a halt, and if the supporting and financial institutions lose belief in the business, the resultant lack of confidence will kill it.

The use of PR within a company might involve such skills as offering stories to the media, being interviewed on TV or radio, making speeches, negotiating sponsorship, planning symposia, seminars, open days or arranging a visit for a VIP. Yet it is the understanding of a total PR commitment that will set the organisation apart. The fixing of a PR objective, which should be communicated and executed downwards throughout the organisation, makes PR a business function that must come under control of the person at the top.

Targeting news

In Chapter 2, we looked at advertising and the way in which, through purchased space in the media, advertising can be quite accurately targeted at a particular audience. PR is used in similar ways but, in the short term, precise targeting is somewhat more difficult to achieve because not everything sent to the media is programmed, PR tends to look at somewhat broader audience definitions. Traditionally PR executives use the word 'publics' which describes the target interest group at which PR editorial is aimed.

David Churchill, consumer affairs correspondent of the *Financial Times*, describes six key target interest groups in which PR can be involved:

- Shareholders and the financial community – to communicate management and financial information, establish credibility, and generate financial support;
- Retailers, wholesalers, and others in the distribution chain – to engender confidence in the organisation's products, services, promotional support, and so on;
- Consumers – both members of the public and industry – to encourage them to use the organisation's products and/or services and to communicate relevant information about the organisation;
- Opinion formers in government – both local and national – to represent the interests of the organisation in legislative terms;
- Local communities – to improve relations in the organisation's neighbourhood, and to help recruitment and staff relations;

- Employees – to help create loyalty and commitment among the workforce.

For all these key groups, bad communications can be disastrous while good communications can be of far-reaching benefit.

Cost-effectiveness

PR activity has become increasingly popular, especially at the local level because it is something that can be quite easily done by the small organisation itself once basic skills are acquired. The popularity of PR is a response by organisations to the need for good communication. PR not only provides the means through which the communication process can be achieved but it has consistently proved itself cheaper and often more cost-effective than other forms of promotion. The viability of a small business will depend crucially on the promotion of the company and its products, but the communication costs of paid advertising can be astronomical.

Remember the Avis 'We try harder' idea? It's more than ten years since Avis, recognising they were not leaders in the car rental market, ran both an advertising and PR campaign saying that as number two in the business they had to put more into their customer service. The PR campaign was brilliantly executed both externally and internally. The fact that trying harder is still associated with Avis really proves the point of how good an effect PR can have on long-term memorability.

What constitutes PR activity

PR is made up of a number of media-centred activities which ensure that news about the organisation and its products reaches the target interest groups. PR activity includes the following:

- Providing news to the media through stories and a news release service
- Making news through events, sponsorship, symposia, debates, meetings, conferences, stunts and exploiting VIP appearances
- Making personal appearances on TV, radio and through public speaking
- Holding open days and factory visits to involve the community
- Practising good citizenship

- Maintaining a customer and advice service
- Getting involved in education by visiting schools, sending out wall charts, etc
- Participating in exhibitions and demonstrations.

Activities should not, however, be carried out on an *ad hoc* basis, they should be part of an overall plan which has targeted objectives. Opportunities should, of course, be exploited but the evolution of the organisation's PR should follow a planned direction with the making of news playing an important role in the overall programme.

Evaluating PR

Unlike sales or advertising campaigns, PR is difficult to measure in quantitative terms. If the organisation is badly hit by adverse publicity, a major accident or a court case, the negative impact of news may reduce business. However, it is difficult to measure incremental business gained by PR. It is probably a good idea to measure PR in two ways:

- First, assess the amount of editorial achieved by PR activity in terms of press cuttings and transcripts from electronic media. This will provide an idea of how effective the PR function is in getting its stories across to the media.
- Second, try to assess the image of the business and its products in the eyes of the targeted interest groups as a result of the company's PR. This may be achieved by observation but will probably be more accurate if assessed by more sophisticated research techniques.

Evaluation of the organisation's PR will help create improvements both in terms of achieving editorial space and through the effect that has on the business in terms of image, confidence and sales. Remember that getting PR is about gaining and winning contacts with the news media. Successful PR people have made it their business to find and build relations with important editors and journalists. The locally based small business will be making a major start when it gets to know the editor of its local paper.

CHAPTER 4
Sales Promotion, Merchandising, Selling and Exhibiting

In this chapter we cover a whole range of exciting activities which in marketing parlance are often dubbed 'below the line activities'. These are activities which are not strictly advertising or PR but all the same play a crucial role in the mix of promotional options.

The following promotional tools are there to sharpen the point of your sales attack:

- Sales promotion activities
- Events
- In-store merchandising
- Telemarketing
- Exhibitions.

These topics are all concerned with gaining *attention*, motivating sales and providing spin-off opportunities for additional publicity.

Sales promotion activities

Sales promotion describes all those activities which, outside PR and advertising, induce people to buy an organisation's products. Sales promotion at trade level may involve special discounts, dealer competitions, competitions for wholesale sales staff or a number of other ideas which would make stockists buy more than usual. Consumer sales promotions involve ideas like 'price offs', coupons, competitions and free samples as well as lots of other ideas to create magic and theatre around a product.

Sales promotion has three basic characteristics:

- It gains attention and often provides information to potential purchasers that helps to stimulate purchase.

Sales Promotion, Merchandising, Selling and Exhibiting

- It incorporates some form of concession, inducement or other form of motivation that gives additional value to the customer.
- It has urgency, inviting the potential buyer to act immediately.

Organisations employ sales promotion to achieve specific tasks such as getting people to make an initial trial of a product or to create a short-term sales response more quickly than long-term image building through advertising – although such an effect is likely to be short-term and may not be effective in building long-term product preference.

Sales promotion can also be used to dramatise a product, particularly one like petrol which is difficult to differentiate.

Types of sales promotion

The types of sales promotion most useful to the small business are:

- Special offers
- Trial offers
- Competitions
- Sponsorship
- Events

Special offers

Special offers can be made either to the *trade* or to *consumers*.

Special offers to the trade include price bonuses, eg 13 items for the price of 12, special discounts linked to purchase volumes, off-seasonal packages, incentives for the trade sales staff, and payments for display or shop window rental.

The reasons for trade special offers may be any of the following:

- To persuade wholesalers and retailers to stock a new product
- To raise trade stock levels ahead of an anticipated sales increase from say advertising or seasonal factors
- To persuade the trade to give your product priority over that of your competitors
- To smooth out ex-factory deliveries in seasonal markets
- As part of a wider deal to involve the trade in a major promotion.

Offers involving price have alongside their many advantages a number of critical drawbacks. Price discounting is so easy that some caution is necessary, for the reasons listed below:

- Too high a stock loading in the trade may result in periods when no orders are received until stocks are cleared
- Slow movement of stocks may result in them reaching the market out of condition
- Dealers may be tardy in settling accounts, thus putting strain on cash flow
- Dealers may insist on returning surplus stocks which may then need cleaning or repacking – which is expensive
- Price discounting may become a habit and thus dealers will expect discounts as a normal part of their trade. When this happens discounts lose their impact, and what is more, continuing discounts may result in a price war with competitors.

Special offers to the consumer, on the other hand, can have a number of benefits:

- Special price offers can be used very effectively in advertising
- Consumers may be encouraged to buy more than normal, thus increasing offtake
- Price promotions may afford the product additional shelf space in retail outlets, thus providing a competitive level of display
- There may be a short-term impact in that consumers may be encouraged to change from their usual product to yours
- There is some news value at point of sale which can be exploited by shelf stickers, or special labels on the pack. The retailer may also wish to advertise the price offer
- Price offers are quick and cheap to mount and are therefore exploitable by the small business.

The disadvantages are:

- Price promotions are all too common and in many marketing areas have lost their impact – they may no longer be so effective
- Internecine price or discount wars have already reduced the profitability of a lot of product categories such as food, household products and clothing. Many price promotions are now defensive tactics against competitors or dictated by major retailers
- There are few opportunities to create any 'magic' around simple price offers.

The most effective use of a price promotion is to support other promotions such as theme promotions.

Trial offers

Inducing consumers, whether they are industrial or members of the general public, to try a new product is an essential task in the adoption process. For the industrial user demonstrations, technical support and free material to experiment with are common. Where a major user is involved, such trial offers should be exploited for every ounce of publicity that can be gained. An article in the industrial press alone may elicit enquiries and the use of an article by sales staff in their sales interviews or mailed to prospects will contribute greatly to a successful sales campaign.

Trial offers to the consumer by way of in-store sampling, door-to-door sampling or special free trials 'money back guaranteed' as a direct response advertisement, are all ways to give the consumer a chance to test the product. The importance of gaining trial among non-users cannot be over-emphasised. Where products are stocked by retailers initial slow offtake may reduce their incentive even to carry the product. This could spell an early demise for a new product if large numbers of retailers discontinue stocking at the same time. Stimulation of demand can be achieved by sampling selectively across a percentage of households in an area: this is often called seeding. During sampling campaigns advertising and PR activity should be running to stimulate awareness and interest, thus enabling the sampling activity to provide the trial stage of the adoption process. Distribution of free samples can be done by professional demonstrators in shops (they have to be well briefed and motivated) or door-to-door by specialised agencies (see Yellow Pages).

Trial offers may also be mounted by banding a trial pack to another item popular among consumers. This practice, common in food-related merchandising, is becoming less popular as many retailers do not wish to participate because of the inconvenience involved. However, on a limited scale such an idea might be adopted by an entrepreneur who finds an opportunity to band his product to one from a major household name.

Competitions

Competitions are the most popular of all types of promotion simply because they enable themes and ideas to be used to dramatise products – particularly those for which it is difficult to prove any great advantage over competitors, eg petrol, baked beans or washing powder. Usually the organisers demand a proof of purchase such as a pack top to encourage a sales response from the promotional idea.

The great theme promotions like Dynasty Money are tremendously expensive, running into millions of pounds and way out of reach of the small business. Yet competitions, from a small raffle at an exhibition to a regional media-backed promotion, are often well within reach.

Use competitions to get people to your stands at exhibitions, to collect business cards, or to get a sales interview.

On a grander scale a deal with a local newspaper to offer anything from a barrel of beer to a Mercedes may well win a lot of media space for the money spent on the prize, as well as a lot of supportive publicity. Such a deal centres around selling a publication on the idea of running a promotional competition based on a theme that will capture the consumer's imagination. The most you will contribute is the prize, supporting material for use at point of sale and often the artwork. The publication will provide space and hype up the promotion through its editorial.

It takes a good idea and a lot of selling, but successfully executed a co-operative promotion of this sort can generate considerable weight both in terms of publicity and response.

A point worth noting is that some 30,000 people are considered to be professional competition entrants. While that may appear to be a ready market they may have little interest in your product and will beg, borrow or even steal whatever you use as a proof of purchase in order to enter.

Because competitions can be dramatised around themes there is considerable scope for creating exciting advertising and display material. Furthermore, lots of opportunities for news stories and pictures can be created. In designing a competition try to look for all the potential opportunities to generate publicity.

Please note that competitions are heavily covered by legal constraints and material should be checked by a lawyer before implementation.

Sponsorship

Today millions are being spent by major companies, particularly in tobacco, banking and insurance, to use the association between sport and themselves and ensure massive publicity. The small business will find it impossible to compete in such an area but by being smart can muscle in quite effectively.

First, as a dealer or franchise it can participate regionally in anything national that its principals care to organise. As a customer or client of the sponsor, why not persuade the organisers to allow you to participate? Make a deal with the sponsors and get a share of the action.

Sales Promotion, Merchandising, Selling and Exhibiting

At a local level there are plenty of opportunities to involve the business in local sponsorship events; sending the local band to a competition, underwriting a swimming gala, running a charity walk, sponsoring the national tiddlywinks competition. Sponsorship brings publicity through those participating, the audience watching and the news that sponsorship events create. Run as much of the action as possible yourself, particularly the PR and advertising, be an active sponsor rather than a passive one and use the attendant publicity for all it's worth. At the same time, you will have lots of fun, you will contribute to the local community (a PR objective in its own right) and you should get lots of publicity. Remember too, exploit sampling and demonstration opportunities at events – you can even have a VIP tent in which to entertain your customers and local dignitaries. Send out press releases to trade and special interest press to widen the publicity net.

Events

From cocktail parties to new product launch conferences, events play a part in both the sales promotion and PR activities of the business. Whether a cocktail party to welcome a foreign buyer is a PR exercise or sales promotion is debatable: but what is not in doubt is that it is an opportunity for publicity.

A small list of common events that the organisation might take advantage of are:

- *Open days*. Let people come in and see what the organisation does. This is not only community PR but it gives the opportunity to show off the organisation's skills and products. What is more there is an opportunity for a news story, at least for the local press.
- *Cocktail parties*. There is always an excuse for a cocktail or lunch-time drinks party. Useful in bringing customers, local officials, media people, or even the staff together. Parties offer an opportunity for speeches, displays and demonstrations of products and of course a press attendance or news release.
- *Conferences* for customers or salesmen can be used to communicate and in the latter case to train and motivate too. Conferences provide a focus for PR generated news, in trade and local press.
- *Hospitality tents and rooms* tend to be the norm at places like Ascot and Wimbledon. For the small business, get invited and do your tendentious socialising at someone else's expense (take plenty of business cards). At local events, where time,

- *Stunts* to draw attention or to get publicity can be useful, particularly at times of the year when there is a dearth of news. Street stunts with clowns and bagpipes, store openings using Miss UK or something unusual at an exhibition can be quite useful in getting a photo caption or a mention. A good stunt may even hit the tabloids.

Events need good organisation. Considerable preparation is therefore essential, so prepare a checklist which should include arranging venues, sending invitations, organising publicity and ensuring printed material is ready on time.

In-store merchandising

The point at which the consumer finds or notices a company's product in a retail outlet is called the *point of sale* (POS). In supermarkets and department stores a great deal of effort goes into making products attractive through good shelving, floor displays and lighting.

Show cards and shelf stickers to attract consumer attention are (in most outlets) carefully sited to prompt customers into purchasing. The material used is called point of sale material. It is at the point of sale that the consumer makes a purchasing decision and the material used is designed to reinforce the consumer's willingness to buy. Here everything the consumer knows, has heard or seen will often be restimulated by a single reminder or an attractive display.

The two elements to discuss therefore are: one, the product pack, and two, POS material.

Product packaging

Packaging has a number of important tasks in building a total product image. It is the front-line presentation for any product, and unattractive packaging will adversely affect product sales. Studies in the US and UK have shown that up to a third of consumers who were pre-sold products by advertising switched to different products when presented with more attractive alternatives.

In presenting a product, packaging has six key tasks:

- attracting consumers at point of sale
- carrying the sales information to point of sale
- projecting the product image

Sales Promotion, Merchandising, Selling and Exhibiting

- providing usage and function information
- providing relevant information demanded by law
- protecting the product.

Attracting consumers at point of sale
The creation of visual impact and purchase appeal is a prime task for packaging, particularly in self-service outlets. First, the packing should tell the consumer what the product is, and second, it should attract attention. Label design should also take into consideration the offerings of competitors with the intention of producing a more attractive and more desirable package.

Carrying the sales information to point of sale
The package has to tell its sales story quickly as consumers will only glance at it. Where mass media advertising permits companies the advantage of pre-selling the product, the package must remind consumers of the sales message at point of sale. It should reinforce the consumer's desire to buy through projecting appeal at point of purchase – for example a food product presents appetite appeal, a consumer durable projects quality and male toiletry products may present masculinity. The package should enable the consumer to identify the product readily.

Packaging is also often required to carry messages for merchandising promotions such as 'price offs', 'competitions' and 'mail ins' to point of sale. These need to stand out in order to attract consumers but they should not devalue the overall attractiveness and communicability of the packaging.

Projecting the product image
The image of a product is an important psychological benefit. Image projection involves considerable aptitude on the part of designers. Consumer testing of package concepts is important in ensuring that the right image is projected.

Providing usage and function information
Most products require some information about usage and function, particularly for technical consumer products and food products. In using the limited space available for such information it is important that the consumer receive the necessary information to be able to use the product successfully. Where instructions on usage are too lengthy or technical in nature the use of a pack insert may be necessary. It is after all essential that the consumer be able to use the product successfully if he or she is to become a regular user.

Providing relevant information demanded by law
The law usually demands the following:

- weight, size or capacity of the products
- safety reminders
- annotations that certain ingredients are present such as in food the presence of antioxidising agents and colorants
- ingredients and formula
- country of origin.

Protecting the product
Protection of the product was undoubtedly the original primary purpose of the package. Today this purpose should not be overlooked or sacrificed in an effort to meet artistic criteria. There is after all little point in producing a product and embellishing it with expensive packaging if it arrives in a retailer's stockroom in an unsaleable condition.

Point of sale material
POS material is both an important point of sales promotion and is also an advertising medium. The closer a sales message can be brought to the point of sale, the more effective it is. Window displays may act in the same way as posters, in-store displays will arrest the consumer's attention and leaflets and show cards will give the potential purchaser that little extra information at the time the purchase decision is being made. Effectively used, POS can often steal a sale from a competitor who is doing all the work to pre-sell consumers and get them along to buy. An example is found in furniture showrooms where purchasers are often attracted away from the advertised brand leader to a little-known name; find the opportunity and test it.

A word of caution, however. Retailers may not share your enthusiasm for placing POS material and may have policies restricting its use: some research is necessary to find out trade attitudes in your sector. Very often retailers will charge for space used and particularly for large window displays. Find out what can be obtained for nothing before agreeing to pay. Remember too that no amount of POS material will induce a customer to buy if your product is out of stock or out of condition on the shelves.

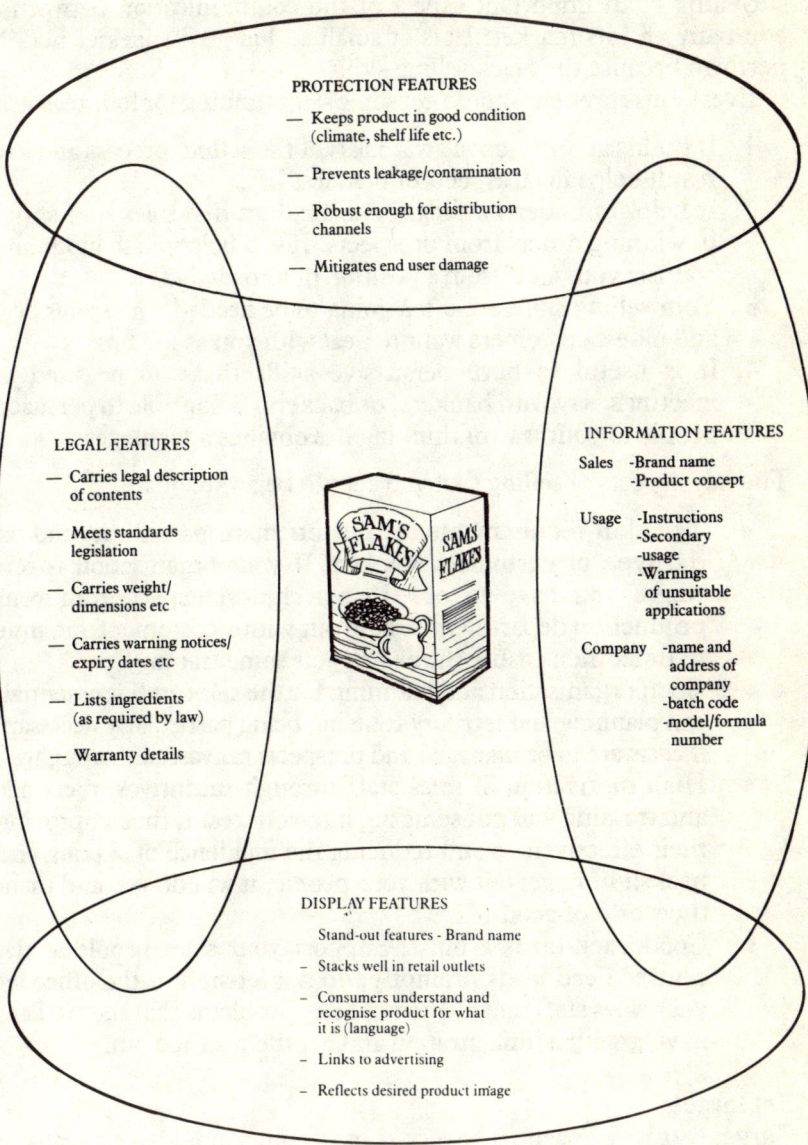

Figure 4.1

Selling

To do full justice to the subject of selling would require a book to itself, so we shall attempt only to outline some key ideas and provide some tips on the subject.

Selling is an important aspect of the communication between a company and its market. Lots of small and large businesses underperform because they lack selling skills.

Every entrepreneur should get some sales training for four reasons:

1. It builds an instinctive awareness of the selling process and as a result helps in all aspects of business life.
2. It helps in understanding the difficulties that sales staff suffer in winning orders from prospects. It will help you to judge and counsel your staff from a position of knowledge.
3. Your selling skills are often going to be needed when your best and oldest customers want to deal with you as the boss.
4. It is useful to have persuasive skills that can be used in meetings, say with bankers, or backers. Being able to persuade people to your way of thinking has obvious advantages.

The key aspects of selling that you should be aware of are:

- The skill requirements in your organisation will depend on the type of customers you see. If your organisation is one where you have to pull in a technical expert from your production department to help out with a customer from time to time, then ensure the expert gets some training.
- Good organisation and planning for the sales staff is essential, call planning and territory routeing being particularly necessary if costs are to be managed and prospects canvassed thoroughly.
- High motivation of sales staff through incentives, meetings and training will put some zip into your team, thus improving their effectiveness and reducing the incidence of skiving and backsliding (get out with your people, it will do you and them the world of good).
- Good back-up is a must. Support your sales people at the centre. Feed leads promptly, do not let staff at the office let your sales staff down. Find out any problems that the staff are having with administration and get them sorted out.

Set targets

Target setting is essential. Every sales person should have a realistic but stretching target. The business as a whole should have a monthly, weekly or even daily sales target against which you can measure your results. Simply setting targets often increases sales because everyone '*just goes for it*', they have something at which to aim. What's important is they have some standard against which to measure themselves.

Benefits of personal selling
Personal selling is found in many forms from a major business negotiation to counter staff in the shop. Yet personal face-to-face selling can have a number of benefits.

- Because it's personal, it allows social relationships to build up between customer and supplier.
- It's flexible and live, allowing the sales person to probe and test the selling proposal before closing the deal with the customer.
- It allows for past mistakes and customer dissatisfaction to be brought out and dealt with during sales interviews.
- The live nature of a tuned-up sales force very often creates a momentum in the business that carries everyone along and builds the business.

Sales force activity should be orchestrated into the overall promotional plan, ensuring that there is harmony between sales objectives and the publicity side of the business. You will read later how to use PR advertising and sales promotion in direct and indirect support of sales force activity. Back your sales staff to the hilt with promotional and administrative support. Motivate and give incentives based on targets, spend time out yourself. Hype everyone up with exciting meetings and straight away your business is going to lift just from the sheer energy you generate.

Telemarketing
Imagine that you could make eight effective sales calls an hour, reaching customers all over the world without actually moving from your office. This is the sort of result that can be achieved by a highly trained telephone selling team and the reason why telemarketing (selling by telephone) is a developing means of reaching customers. Using the telephone to sell has a lot of obvious benefits for the small business. The telephone, for example, allows you to make many more sales calls on customers at a lower cost than you could possibly do by personal visits, yet still maintain the intimate nature of a sales

interview. It is, however, often said that telephone selling is less effective than 'eyeball to eyeball' negotiation, yet the volume of successful calls at a relatively low cost can turn the argument in favour of the phone.

The phone used effectively can increase the geographical size of your market. From an office at home you can contact people all over the world. The phone offers three advantages over personal calling:

- Volume of sales calls can be very much higher
- Costs of calls are lower than personal visits
- The unlimited size of the market available to you.

The telephone is used in a number of ways to aid the sales attack:

- To gather intelligence. Phone prospects to find out who is the right person to deal with. Find out current suppliers, types of material used, etc
- Make appointments by phone. This not only saves the costs of unproductive cold calls but ensures that you meet the right person
- Use the phone for the sales interview – *with training* you can become very effective. You can still see your most important customers, but why not use the phone to pick up business from more marginal customers?
- Follow-ups to visits can be done by phone – this is cheaper than a visit yet still more intimate than a letter
- Use the phone to pick up routine orders
- Use the phone as a customer service medium
- Use the phone to chase up debtors and for handling routine service matters with customers.

Training in telephone selling is important. There are a number of establishments which can get you or your staff up to an effective standard.

Telephone sales campaigns can be contracted out to telemarketing specialists. These contractors have reputations to maintain and employ skilled telephone sales people. The advantages are that at least a proportion of the fee can be result-based and that, like direct response advertising, the service can be turned on and off as you decide. The main disadvantage is that you have very little control over the way these telemarketing companies project your image. They may well be effective in getting business for you yet their approach can often be somewhat abrasive which may be off-putting to some potential customers.

Exhibitions

The exhibition has been left to the end of this pot pourri of sales promotion activities because it is a rather specialised subject. Here we hope to offer a few pointers in the direction of successful exhibiting.

Exhibitions are a popular way of promoting the company and its products. There are two sorts of exhibition, trade and consumer. The benefits of regularly exhibiting at trade shows are in getting to know the key buyers, making trade contacts, and seeing what the competition is offering; these benefits are over and above any business contracted during the show. Consumer exhibitions provide the opportunity to show and demonstrate products to consumers, and apart from the millions of little boys who seem to revel in collecting brochures, there is an opportunity to reach and influence consumers interested in what you have to offer.

In looking at successful exhibiting therefore, we shall outline a number of key points that will help.

Why exhibit? Most organisations do not exhibit simply because they have not thought about it. Some may never have even visited an exhibition despite years of trading. One cure for this is to take time out and make visits to relevant exhibitions – you can find out about them in the *Exhibition Bulletin* or from your trade press.

For those embarking on exhibiting for the first time, here are a few useful tips:

- Select very carefully the exhibitions in which you intend participating. Follow the trade, use the ones which the brand leaders in your sector favour. Visit a few before deciding – that means thinking up to 12 months ahead. Visit stands and talk to exhibitors.
- Decide why you want to exhibit and who you want to meet. Set some objectives:
  — launch a new product
  — find distributors or agents
  — launch a franchise
  — let the trade know you are seriously in business.
- Get information. Good exhibitions will provide lists of exhibitors and breakdowns by number and type of previous exhibition visitors. Study information provided and find the exhibitions best suited to you and try to visit them.
- Booking major exhibitions up to a year in advance may be necessary, although sometimes good discounts can be obtained

- at the last minute if an exhibitor has pulled out or there is other space available.
- The exhibition organisers will rent you space and not much more. It will be up to you to design and equip your stand. Remember that the exhibition will have a finite number of visitors and that, regardless of how large a stand you have, you will not increase the number of people passing through the turnstiles. Enquiries, however, tend to be in proportion to the amount of frontage, thus corner stands tend to be more expensive. Do not book stands in areas where visitor traffic is low, go for places near toilets or the bars.
- Design your stand properly. There is a great temptation for new exhibitors to design their own. A professionally designed stand is better lit and more pleasant to look at. Display your most interesting exhibits where passers-by can see them. Never use damaged items or prototypes; they will not create the right image. Instead use models of your material if necessary to display and demonstrate your product. Avoid steps on to the stand as this tends to put people off, and be practical.
- Staff the stand with people who know the products being exhibited and who have been trained to sell. Beautiful girls hired from a model agency may attract customers, but if they cannot hold their interest through technical discussion, contracts will not be made.

Staff behaviour is critical to a successful exhibition.

- Do not let them get into huddles that ignore prospective customers.
- Do not sit unless you want a potential customer to sit (one way of holding his attention).
- Do not eat, drink or smoke on the stand, it creates a bad impression and it also makes a mess.
- Keep staff alert by rotating their periods of duty and ensure that they get fresh air and meals. Difficult as it is, try to avoid late night exhibition drinking bouts; save that for the last night.
- Do not try to run an exhibition on your own or just with your spouse. It's exhausting and a divorce or nervous breakdown is not going to help you or the business.

Attract passers-by by making the stand interesting and providing something that will get them to stop and take notice. A charming young lady standing in the gangway with a free raffle works over and over again and it is a really good method of collecting business cards.

Other ideas can include audio-visual displays, TVs showing sporting events, competitions, wheels of fortune, running water and so on – anything that gives movement and life to a stand will make it competitive with the hundreds of others in the same exhibition.

Approaching prospects is a skill that needs to be learned and practised. Too often the prospect is turned away because either staff are too eager or too ignorant. Never jump on someone who steps on the stand. Do not make visitors uncomfortable by watching them but do not let them slip away by ignoring them. Try the following: let people browse around until their attention is arrested then say, for example, 'let me show you how this works', or 'are you aware of our new range?' Never say 'May I help you?' There is no answer if the prospect says no.

Keep names and addresses in a visitors book and do not lose it. Send brochures and other material directly to the prospect's office or home. Type the label there and then and stick it on enveloped material ready for the purpose. The prospect will receive your brochure in the morning when he or she has left everyone else's on the train.

Give everyone your business card (which is of normal size and will fit a business card wallet and not get lost) and keep every one given to you. An exhibition is a place to make all sorts of contacts; customers, suppliers, agents, designers, advertising agencies, foreign trade delegates and so forth. Your presence, your material and your staff are there to make the most of the opportunities provided. It's here that the industry press article you had published in the trade press before the exhibition is going to be useful when talking to people about your product and company. Keep your camera to hand to record that bit of commercial serendipity when Princess Margaret visits your stand; be the first to get your photograph into the trade press and your local papers.

After the exhibitions your work really begins. First, all the contacts made have to be followed up quickly before their interest wanes. Press releases on anything that can be considered as newsworthy such as sales or interest in a new line, a spectacular order, an order from abroad, should go out to the relevant media; letters to contacts following up discussions should go out, as should a mail shot to contacts who either sought information or who left their cards. A little overkill here will not be very expensive and a single order will probably cover the costs.

One word of warning: your first exhibition might not be as rewarding as you anticipate. Exhibiting is a bit like moving into a new neighbourhood where getting to know people takes time. Use your first exhibition to introduce yourself and your company and to make both trade and customer contacts. Keep the exhibition catalogue for your records, to remind you next year who participated in your sector and who did not. Look each year for absentees, particularly among close competitors or the big brand people, and muscle into the gap they leave.

CHAPTER 5
Designing Press Advertisements

Advertising must be persuasive if it is to have any real effect and this point must be remembered when designing an advertisement. You are in the business of making your advertisements sell your products or company services. So avoid being smart and gimmicky. Keep your advertisements clear, simple and persuasive, and above all be objective about what you are trying to achieve.

Press advertisements have to compete with both the editorial and other advertisements for the reader's eye so your advertisement will need certain qualities to enable it to:

- stand out and attract attention
- hold the reader's interest
- convey a simple selling proposition quickly
- create desire in the reader's mind
- tell the reader how or where to buy the product.

Evaluate every advertisement you produce by asking yourself if it follows these lines. Study advertisements in the press and evaluate them too. Try and see what makes them effective – because not all are!

To produce good and effective press advertisements two stages of development are required:

1. Produce a creative strategy (ie a strategy involving your selling proposition, your market position and target reader).
2. Design the advertisement around the creative strategy. This is called a creative execution.

Develop a creative strategy

A creative strategy is a term devised by advertising people to describe the way in which the elements of an advertising campaign are going to be focused in order to persuade the market to respond.

In designing advertisements therefore the creative strategy will dictate what is required of the advertisement in terms of its message for the potential customers to whom it is targeted.

There are basically two elements to consider in building a creative strategy which produces an advertisement which will successfully appeal to the target consumer and these are:

- find a *selling proposition* for the product
- dramatise *the proposition* through design and creativity.

In producing a creative strategy then, go for the following:

- find a unique *point of difference* between your products and other offerings on the market
- find a *position*, niche or segment in the market, which values your unique point and difference, that can be profitably exploited – this is your target market
- define the characteristics of potential customers within the segment you intend to position – these will be your target readers.

Find a unique feature of your product or service

In finding and developing a *selling proposition* for your product the more clearly you can differentiate your offering from that of your competitors the greater the chance that you will be successful with advertising and selling the product. You should therefore seek differences in your product that can be used to appeal to potential buyers.

By evaluating the features or benefits of your product you may find that some may be:

- different from your competitors
- better than your competitors
- unique to the market.

You should therefore list all the advantages and features of your product in order to find *points of difference* between your product and those of your competitors. Here some lateral thinking might be

Designing Press Advertisements

of benefit to avoid what I describe as the *product maker's mindset*, ie the mental view that most people have about the products they themselves make and sell. Your mindset is probably quite different from that of your customers, so make your list of features by evaluating your product along lines similar to those listed below:

The product	*Your product*	*Competitors*
Features		
Sizes		
Standardised or custom made		
Colours		
Latest model		
Quality end of market		
Cheap end of market		
Featured on TV		
Voted best in the *Observer*		
Easy to fit		
Folds away		
Price		
Inexpensive		
Discounts		
Premium/quality		
Payment facilities		
Credit plans		
Service		
Guarantees/warranties		
Fitting		
Advice centres		
Free estimates		
Expert advice		
After sales service		
200 years in business		
Endorsements		
Available in Boots and all leading chemists		
Open on Mondays		
Special offers		
Prime promotion		
Other promotion		
Free trial		

List your features and benefits and see if anything obvious appears that makes your product seem better than the competitors' or offers something entirely unique to the market. Now look at your target market and relate the features back to them. Do they have a relevant value to your buyers' needs? Which has relevance to your market? Which will appeal? Which will present the best opportunity to gain attention, stimulate interest and build a desire to buy? Look again and again, brainstorm ideas with your colleagues and friends until you find that magical point of difference.

Your product has to be seen by the reader as special. The identification of what advertising people call a *unique selling point* (USP) for your product will make the difference in the way it is seen in the consumer's eyes.

Position your product

Finding your product's points of difference enables you to assess its potential against those of your competitors. You now need to find a position in the market where your product best meets the needs of your potential customers.

Assess the potential of the position or segment you wish to occupy and decide whether it is commercially right for you or not. If not you have to try again to find a better position. To attack the competition in your market position and at the same time trawl other segments with alternative propositions which might appeal to neighbouring segments would be an ideal strategy, but your principal objective would be to occupy and defend the segment of the market you decided would be the best for you.

Target audience

Your analysis and evaluation of your product so far will have given you your USP and your positioning in the market. The next step will be to find out who your potential customers are. Here some research will be of value and this will depend on how well you know your own market and how specialised your product is. You do, however, need to have some idea of your target readers along the lines described in Chapter 1.

You will find that through your advertising, experience of your market will grow and you will get to know more about your target readers as you go. The problem for the first-time advertiser is in being fairly accurate about the target audience from the outset – otherwise a

Designing Press Advertisements

lot of money can be wasted before sufficient knowledge and experience of the market can be acquired. If your advertisements fail it will be for one of two reasons:

- the selling proposal had no appeal to the readers
- the advertisements failed to reach the target market.

It goes without saying therefore that you should constantly be monitoring the progress of your advertising through customer records, research and trade knowledge and that you should be forever building a picture of your customers – bearing in mind that they will change as time progresses, as will your competition and trade channels.

So what do you have so far?

- A unique selling point
- A position
- A target audience.

With this knowledge you are now in a position to put together a creative strategy statement. The example below illustrates the point.

Creative execution of the strategy

Take your creative strategy statement and begin to play around with ways of making an advertisement from it. Obviously an advertising agency could take up the job from here, so might a designer, but if you are attempting the job yourself this is the time to start being creative.

Visualise

Visualise your statement, scribble down ideas as they come to you and then evaluate the ideas against your creative strategy statement. Do not try to fine-tune your ideas or write copy initially, just produce rough outlines (unless a stroke of genius gives you the headline you are looking for). To some people the ideas may come quickly, others may experience difficulties. Try bouncing ideas backwards and forwards with a colleague, spouse or friend.

Develop

The next step is to develop your ideas into an advertisement. Take your rough visuals and ask yourself which treatment is simplest in terms of putting over the selling proposition and which will be most easily understood by, and interesting to, the target reader. Begin to develop the idea that strikes you best and work it up until you have something around which to base a design.

Design

The advertisement will have two basic elements – *illustrations and words*. The design of the advertisement therefore will be based on getting these two elements to work together to put across the creative strategy.

Illustration

The illustration can be used to:

1. gain attention – by using an unusual, interesting or humorous picture;
2. give atmosphere – by setting the scene in terms of time, place and character;
3. provide emotional stimulus – by using a picture that will appeal to the emotions;
4. provide visual information – in terms of size, shape and numbers.

Words

The words are of great importance in an advertisement and bear the brunt of the strategy in terms of persuading the reader to act. We can divide them into:

Headline. To gain attention. (Often subheadings are used to hold the reader's attention and to break up the copy.)

Introduction. In order to relate the headline to the rest of the advertisement and, at the same time, stimulate the reader's interest in the advertisement, we need a brief introduction.

Description. The description provides the reader with the relevant information on which he can base his decision.

Demand for action. As we have seen previously, our advertising needs to demand action.

Tell the reader how to take up the offer. Again we must give the reader sufficient information to take up the offer.

Writing the copy

The next stage in designing a press advertisement is to write the copy, the length and scope of which will be influenced by:

1. *The total size*. This will govern the maximum number of words that we can use.
2. *The size and task of the illustration*. Naturally, we can suppose that the space available is that left after the illustration is in place. When regarding the relative importance of each we should consider why we have included an illustration. If it is purely to attract attention, then we will obviously need more copy to describe our proposition. If, on the other hand, the illustration provides a great deal of the information then our copy can be briefer. Remember the picture will do a lot of the communicating both in terms of illustrating the product offered and in dramatising it.

Producing the headline
To produce a headline we should consider that:

1. It should attract favourable attention; it must be relevant to the subject and should not be offensive to the target audience, otherwise it will antagonise the reader and reduce the effectiveness of the advertisement.
2. It should expose the subject advertised only to the necessary degree. There are two basic ground rules for dealing with this problem:
    - If we are advertising something which is constantly in demand and our principal problem is to get the reader to take up our proposition rather than someone else's, then we can expose the subject in the advertisement. Such examples are found in advertising foodstuffs, shoes and detergents.
    - If we are advertising something which is likely to produce resistance, or a reluctance to become interested, on the part of the reader (such as giving to charity or even joining an organisation), we should be less overt. In other words, produce a headline which in itself will capture the reader's attention in order that he will begin to assimilate the message.

To save spending hours trying to think up a suitable headline, we can look at the following three types, and fit one to our creative strategy.

Types of headline
A question headline. The result of asking the reader a question will take him through a mental process of trying to answer it. This attracts

the reader's attention and puts him into an enquiring frame of mind. Questions are the easiest form of effective headline to fit the creative strategy. For example, 'How much did you spend on heating last year?'

A statement headline. Statement headlines are useful in that they can be made to make the reader curious. Even if the reader disputes the statement there is a fair chance that the advertisement will be read in an effort to prove himself right.

'Act now' headline. A popular use of this kind of headline is by retailers: 'Last week of sale' or 'Hurry, only a few left at this price.' These are useful for the organisation advertising an event: 'Hurry! your last chance.' This type of headline, although limited in its application, is useful where it can be employed, as it works on the human desire of 'not wanting to be left out'.

Producing the body copy

This section includes the introduction and the description. In writing this we must go through three stages:

Stage 1. Plan the argument. Plan a mental argument through which the reader is led to see himself enjoying the benefits of what is advertised; and at the same time give the reader sufficient information on which to base a decision.

Stage 2. Pre-empt objections. We must pre-empt any objections the reader may put up to the proposition. This is done by a rational appraisal of what resistance the reader is likely to have to the proposition. Remember, we would not need to advertise if people were as sold on the idea as we are; thus we need to put ourselves in the reader's position to work out possible objections. Say, for example, we were advertising a course on mountain-climbing; we might foresee the reader's objections as:

- mountain-climbing is dangerous;
- it requires fitness;
- it requires expensive equipment.

We could pre-empt these objections by saying:

- you start off on the safe rocks;
- we appreciate it takes time for you to get fit, so the course takes account of this;
- all equipment is provided in the total price.

Thus we reduce the reader's immediate resistance to our advertisement by putting his mind at rest, putting him into a more responsive frame of mind.

Stage 3. List points. Having planned the argument and examined the reader's probable objections, our next task is to list the points in their order of presentation. The statements should start by relating the copy to the headline, and lead up to the 'demand for action' statement.

There is little point in developing a persuasive argument unless we actually tell the reader what we want him to do. The potential respondent will be in a receptive mood if our copy has done its job, and we need to make the reader act on the information provided.

We can produce a 'demand for action' statement as:

A challenge. Examples: 'Now ignore us if you can', or 'If you are the man you think you are, join us.'

One of the oldest methods of motivating people into taking action is the challenge. Generals have won victories and men have climbed mountains for dares.

A question. Example: 'Are you man enough to take it?'

To question the reader's physique, virility, intelligence etc is again a powerful way of motivating response as it works on his vanity.

A plea. Examples: 'Power to help is in your hands', or 'Please give generously.'

A plea is an excellent way of ending an emotions-based advertisement in that it gives the reader a sense of self-satisfaction in taking up the proposition.

A command. Examples: 'Cut out this coupon and fill it in now', or 'Call for free estimate.'

This form of statement needs powerful, urgent copy to make it work, in that all resistance to act by the reader must be broken down by the preceding copy.

Further information

Finally we need to give the reader the means of taking up the offer. We can do this in a number of ways:

- provide a coupon reply;
- provide an address;
- provide a telephone number;
- give other instructions relevant to the subject of the advertisement, for example tell the customer how to take up the offer: ('available at Boots and other leading chemists').

It is always worth providing alternative instructions, for example 'Call', 'Telephone' or 'Send the coupon below'. Remember, the easier it is for the reader to take up the offer the more likely he is to respond.

We can now put our copy together. It will probably mean that we shall need to write it out several times before we get it just how we want it.

Further notes on copy

The copywriter needs to have some knowledge of how the human mind works. The enthusiast might borrow the odd book on psychology but will probably find that he or she can learn more by observing his fellow human beings. Sheer experience shows that people respond differently to different stimuli. For example, the football coach who constantly reminds his team that they are 'hopeless' is unlikely to motivate them into winning the next match. Yet the patient teacher can gain results from his students by encouragement and praise.

The secret of successful copywriting stems from the following:

1. studying the target audience and correctly assessing its needs;
2. creating a mental picture in which the reader can see himself;
3. concentrating the direction and flow of the copy, concisely, with vitality and vigour and, above all, with conviction;
4. using a style which flows easily (which is not too slick) and which provides a character and personality for the subject.

Consider these two examples of copy written for two different types of jacket produced for different sorts of people.

> A man's jacket; styled in a rugged tweed. Just right for an afternoon on a chilly trout stream.
>
> This denim-look jacket, styled for a night on the town.

We have done away with long descriptions, but the character of each jacket is easily transmitted to the reader. What is more the reader could actually see himself enjoying the benefits of either.

Style

The question of writing in an effective style is a difficult point to put over in a few words, but we can look at the two extremes which the reader of this book should avoid.

Too stiff. Our well-known photographic service is again available to cover your wedding requirements this spring. We undertake colour work . . .

Too slick. This fantastic slim-line washing machine sits snugly in your kitchen. Ladies, you'll love its super-touch button controls. It spins washing . . .

We can improve our copywriting by analysing and criticising as many advertisements as possible. See how many you can improve.

Selecting a designer
An advertising agency
An advertising agency is the obvious choice because their designers have tremendous knowledge and skill in press design. However, if you are not employing an agency then it will be very difficult if not highly expensive to persuade them to do the graphic design for your advertisement. If you are doing your own advertising then you will probably have to find an alternative to an agency.

A commercial artist
When commissioning an artist, ask to look at the artist's portfolio to see what sort of work he or she does. In the provinces many artists are 'jacks of all trades', producing a variety of work. In London, however, many specialise in different aspects of their field and even if they accept your brief they may be totally unsuitable.

Advertisement design facilities
Many evening and local newspapers have facilities to cater especially for small-budget advertisers (from whom they gain about half their earnings). If you provide the copy and some ideas on how the ad should look, then they will produce it for you.

Many publications provide free copy and design facilities and many (but not all) produce very good results. You will, of course, have to place an advertisement in the publication but they will give you back the artwork for use elsewhere.

To find out whether the papers in your area provide such facilities, look them up in the Yellow Pages or *British Rate and Data* and telephone the advertising manager to find out.

Produce the components yourself
This is the least-recommended method, but if the publication has no free design facilities, it may be an alternative. Take along the copy and, say, photographs you intend to use, plus a rough layout, to the publication in which you are going to advertise. They will put the

components together (as best they can) and will send you a 'pull' for approval. (A 'pull' is a printed-up version of the advertisement supplied by the printers, prior to publication.)

Produce professional advertisements – ALWAYS

When a text such as this is written it is very easy to give the impression that advertisements can be produced to a formula, and that results will be perfect every time. Advertisement production should never become an automatic piecemeal operation; each should be individually produced to be effective and persuasive. What has been said in this chapter should be viewed as a discipline and to it the reader can add his own creative flair and that of his colleagues. Work should always turn out aesthetically pleasing and should be objectively examined to find possible weaknesses and faults that will put the potential respondent off.

Look at as many advertisements as you can; judge them, and try to improve them. Take the advice of professional advertising people and designers and never accept second-rate work. It should always be remembered that the more effective the advertisement is, the higher the response will be. In fact, most media planners will agree that money spent on preparing the advertisement to the highest possible standard, for the campaign might be better spent than increasing the weight of delivery.

Naturally, you have to temper this with good sense and responsibility to ensure that the basic planning requirements are fulfilled, but this view is worth bearing in mind when allocating the budget. The advertisements reproduced on pages 57 and 65 are examples of effective advertising which brought in a very good response from the public.

Briefing the designer and checking artwork

Simply asking a designer to produce an advertisement is not the way to get good results. For no matter how good the designer is, he will not be able to interpret your ideas unless you brief him adequately.

Before the designer can even begin to start work you need to provide him with:

1. overall dimensions of the advertisement;
2. the width of the columns for the publication in which we are going to advertise (obtainable from the publication's advertisement manager);
3. the process restrictions (for example, limited use of colour);

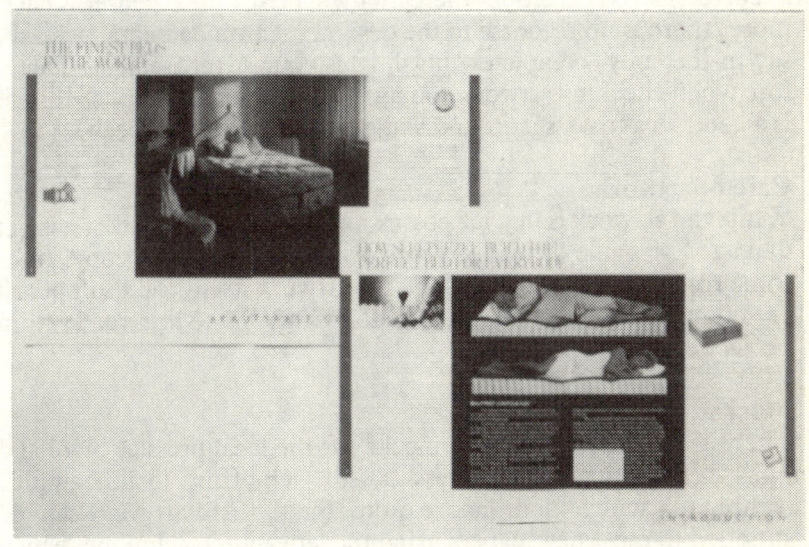

Figure 5.1
By permission of Cushion Kilminster Skudder Ltd

4. A sample or samples of the publication you intend using. This lets the designer see what reproduction weaknesses there are, and allows him to compensate accordingly.
5. Go through your rough sketches (scamps) and ideas with the designer for him to interpret what is in your mind.
6. Let the designer read the copy. It would be a good idea to talk through your creative intentions to ensure that the designer fully understands what you are trying to achieve.

Stages of producing artwork

Stage 1. The designer will usually want to be sure that you are in agreement with his interpretation of the brief. He will therefore produce one or two rough sketches of his ideas and will ask for approval.

Stage 2. The designer will then 'mock up' the advertisement so that you can see what the finished job will look like. At this stage you can still make fundamental changes to the design without incurring extra costs; thereafter costs will be very high.

Stage 3. Having gained approval of the mock up, the designer will produce finished artwork. It is your responsibility to check it for mistakes, because the designer will then ask you to sign the artwork as correct. Any corrections thereafter will be at your expense. What is more, there is no recourse to the designer if a fundamental mistake, say in the copy, completely invalidates your advertisement. Therefore when checking artwork you must check every single word and it is a good idea to pass it around and get other people to check it too.

Care of artwork

While the artwork is in your possession you must ensure that it is not damaged or made dirty. Do your corrections on a photocopy. If for some reason you have to work on the artwork itself, use a soft pencil or you may scratch and damage it. If artwork has to be remade it can be very expensive.

Blocks

There is no need to produce blocks for the local press as more and more are turning to a process called 'web-offset' (a lithographic technique) which does not require them. Flat artwork can be supplied to most newspapers using the letterpress technique, which requires blocks and they will produce blocks on your behalf. (Many charge very little for this service these days and, in any event, you can always bargain.)

Other types of press advertisement

Many organisations do not need to produce expensive illustrated display advertisements, some don't have the money to invest and others may need to produce non-display advertisements in support of their campaigns or in media such as the Yellow Pages. Let us look now at some other types of advertisement.

Classified advertisements

Classified advertisements present us with three limiting factors:

1. it is difficult to gain attention;
2. there are no illustrations;
3. the copy has to be brief.

In expressing your creative strategy, these three restrictions have to be borne in mind and therefore you must examine your ideas to ensure that they can be simply communicated. However, to some extent you can overcome these problems by looking more closely at what the classified columns can offer:

- white space;
- different sizes and density of type face.

So in producing a classified advertisement you can use a combination of white space, print size and density to gain attention. (Look at the example shown below.) Introduce a heading in bold capital letters and use white space to break up the matter and make it more pleasing to look at.

SAVE CENTRAL HEATING COST

By having central heating fitted now,
in summer, you can save up to 25 per cent.
Phone John Greene now for a free
estimate on 0677 5592214.

JOHN GREENE HEATING

(REGISTERED CORGI GAS INSTALLER)

The copy
In the above example we can divide our copy into five basic parts:

Heading. This not only introduces the message but is also used to capture the reader's attention. We could use a question such as: ARE

YOU A MAN?; or a bold statement such as WINDSURFERS WANTED; DEAD ON TIME; or FURNITURE WANTED to attract the reader's eye to the advertisement.

Description. The next stage is to make brief descriptions of what is offered, using the few words that space allows to make the reader see himself getting benefit, rather than throwing random statements at him.

Demand for action. Following the description we must demand action with a firm statement; for example, 'Phone now', 'Call today'. The reason for this is that, having put the reader into the frame of mind to consider the proposition, we need to get him to act urgently; otherwise he will put off his decision and maybe forget.

Tell the reader how to take up the offer. Having demanded his action, we must give the reader sufficient information to enable him to do what is required. Here a phone number is useful in that it saves words (if possible provide the name of the person receiving enquiries by telephone; having someone to ask for gives the respondent assurance and overcomes any shyness or hesitancy).

Endorsement. Classified advertisements are not always trusted by the public so it helps to slip in a single endorsement to indicate your *bona fides* eg 'Registered Corgi Gas Installer'.

Semi-display advertisement

The term 'semi-display' implies that we can take advantage of some display facilities. Design elements are pretty basic, such as frames, line drawings, display lettering and so forth. We can use these to help attract the reader's eye.

The copy follows on the same lines as classified advertisements but the semi-display presentation will stand out much more effectively.

Advertisements without illustrations

We can develop a semi-display type of advertisement to produce effective half-page or even whole-page advertisements. With as few words as possible and barely any other design elements we can produce an advertisement with lots of impact.

This type of advertisement is particularly useful for announcing major events or supporting political campaigns. Again no artwork is required from the organisation as the publication will make up the advertisement.

Advertising features (Advertorials)

Here again is a method of producing an advertisement which requires little or no artwork by the organisation. Advertising features are advertisements produced to look like any other page of editorial. They have certain advantages for new product launch campaigns, or as part of a public relations plan. They look like a page of news and therefore carry a certain conviction.

We can usually get the publication to make up the advertisement and they will provide a journalist to write the copy if need be. Let us briefly break the production process into three stages: copy, design and additional activities.

Copy
Very often copy for the advertising feature is written as an article, seemingly doing nothing to persuade the reader. We could have produced an article and had it published for nothing as part of our public relations exercise. Therefore, when we produce an advertisement feature we should look back at our creative strategy and interpret it for this type of advertisement. The copy should be broken down into a series of headings and we can then use these to produce a series of shorter stories (in the same way as a newspaper breaks up its major news stories). This has the advantage that the reader does not have to plough through a long article, and if we plan our headings for each article, we can use them to précis our total message.

Design
The design of the advertorial requires:

1. Visual impact from good graphic design for the total advertisement; that is, striking headline, good concise layout using contrast of bold and light type as well as prominent subheadings:
2. Interesting photographs which are used to attract attention and to supply visual information;
3. Additional semi-display advertisements to put over individual messages (see below).

Additional activity
For an advertorial feature of half a page upwards, we can also use some of the space to insert one or two semi-display advertisements. These are not used to clutter the advertisement but to help break the typescript and provide the reader with additional information.

One extra tip when using advertising features: get extra copies run off for use at exhibitions or for your sales staff to use.

Don't forget to support your press advertising with PR releases to add credibility and to widen the reach of your campaign.

CHAPTER 6
Designing Posters and Leaflets

The need for a creative strategy is not confined to press advertising. Finding the best way of appealing to a target audience is just as important in other types of advertisement, for example posters. The difficulties of extending creative strategies into other forms of advertising are, by and large, the design limitations of less flexible media. Yet *posters*, *leaflets* and *direct mail* do have a number of physical advantages over press advertising and can be used for attaining specific objectives or to supplement press activities. The main advantage is that you can control distribution. Posters, for example, can be used to boost advertising in very specific geographical areas. Leaflets and direct mail can be targeted at very specific audiences.

As suggested in the previous chapter, your creative strategy should be designed with both the target audience and the chosen medium in mind. Sometimes you will find that your ideal strategy, which might be perfectly suited to press advertising, might be difficult to interpret with, say, posters or direct mail. Thus, some compromise must be made if the strategy is to be interpreted through other media.

Posters

Although hand-produced posters can play an important role in the organisation's publicity programme, the need for professional design when producing printed posters is as necessary as with press advertising. Professional assistance can come from the same source as for the press (excepting newspapers' design facilities) and the printer might handle fairly straightforward jobs (especially if he happens to specialise in posters).

This extremely useful and flexible form of advertising is so often put at a disadvantage by poor design. The principal reason stems from a lack of awareness of how posters convey their message. First, if you view poster advertising from the position of your audience you will immediately see that any one poster competes for attention with the hustle and bustle of the streets: the traffic, shop windows, noisy children. Distractions are abundant and unfortunately the better the site (that is, the larger the flow of pedestrian traffic which circulates around it) the greater the distractions. You might also remember that, as with any other form of advertisement, your message will have to compete with other people's advertising and with readers' priorities. Nobody goes past a poster site with the deliberate intention of reading the poster, with the possible exception of sites near bus stops and at railway stations etc where the reader might want to avert boredom.

Regardless of whether the poster is produced by hand or printed, its effectiveness depends on whether it is both *noticed and understood*.

Thus, hurriedly scribbled or overworded posters are considerably less effective than those which use simple design elements, contrasting colours and bold, easily read lettering.

You might well view your production of hand-drawn posters from the point of view of quality rather than quantity; one good poster, well sited, might gain a greater response than ten badly produced. Ask yourself if they can be easily read and understood from a distance and whether they deliver a persuasive message.

Designing posters

Having emphasised the need for a simple design which will arrest the reader's attention, you should look at how you can achieve effective poster design. First, let us consider posters which are going to be professionally designed and printed, where you are more motivated to achieve maximum effectiveness because you will be obliged to spend a portion of your coveted budget. As with press advertising, you can produce advertisements which consist of *words only* or a mixture of *words and illustrations*.

Depending on the money available you might also add to the impact through the dimension of colour.

The more words you cram into your poster the less effective it will become. Yet you should aim to provide the reader with adequate information on which to base and carry out a decision.

In producing an argument you will have to resort to using either a single complete statement which completely encapsulates the message (which is usual when posters are used to support other advertising) or use a series of bold statements which make up the offer.

The design should be visually attractive, allowing the reader's eyes to sweep rapidly over the words. Stand-out can be achieved by:

1. *Bold lettering*. Try to read the poster from 25 yards.
2. *Contrasting colours*. For example, blue words/orange background, primary red on green, black on white, but never yellow, orange or green on white.
3. *Absence of trivial elements*. The cleaner the design the better it stands out.
4. *Above all*: A SIMPLE MESSAGE.

Added value of an illustration

Provided that an illustration can be produced to increase the attention-gaining qualities of the poster, you can use it to help the quality of your message by creating atmosphere, credibility and character. Look at the Oxfam poster on page 65 whose message consists of a single word. The illustration says all that is needed.

If you beware of using illustrations that become dull, date or are offensive and instead, illustrate as a device to attract attention and to save words, then the effectiveness of the poster design is going to be greatly improved. Avoid trivial embellishments simply to fill in the spaces between the words, because in creating impactful designs those empty spaces contribute to the overall effect.

You might do well to keep your eyes open for posters, whether produced by voluntary organisations, public services or industry, and examine them for strengths and weaknesses. There is one thing about publicity; you can plagiarise other people's good ideas and modify them for your own benefit.

Hand-produced posters

A carefully done, hand-drawn poster can be as effective as its printed counterpart and have the great advantage of costing virtually nothing.

Spirit-based felt markers are the ideal tools for the job and these can be obtained in a number of colours. They are simple to use and their broad tip allows the ink to flow generously on to the paper. Make the letters large and bold and keep the message short. Once again, do not embroider the white spaces with trivia; it serves no purpose and reduces effectiveness. Test the stand-out qualities by viewing the finished poster from a distance.

Figure 6.1 *An Oxfam poster. A single word and a powerful illustration serve to convey at a glance all that needs to be said.* (Courtesy of Oxfam)

There are a number of ways of speeding up the production of hand-produced posters; these might include the use of a hand-made printing screen or stencils.

One imaginative local trader in our area invented a method: he cut out letters in cardboard, laid them down on a sheet of white paper, and sprayed the whole area with an aerosol paint. When the paint was dry the letters were removed, leaving a striking poster of white letters reversed out of colour. The paint takes only a few minutes to dry, thus permitting a good number of posters to be made in a very short time.

Limitations of posters

Long messages are difficult to put over by poster advertising. So too are subjects which are totally unfamiliar to the reader. This is because lengthy explanations are likely to be required in order to provide sufficient information on which the reader can base a decision.

This does not mean, however, that posters cannot be used to support, say, a press campaign for a subject which requires lengthy explanation. In such a case you would use posters to remind the public of what has been said in the press campaign.

Leaflets

The basis of producing illustrations and copy follow, in broad terms, the guidelines for display advertisements, listed in Chapter 5. However, before you produce your leaflet, you should first consider the purpose for which it is required.

You could produce different leaflets for your various tasks, such as an inexpensive one-colour handbill for bulk distribution, or you could spend a lot of money on a prestige booklet to commemorate an event or for use as a catalogue.

The design of the leaflet should be placed in the hands of the professional designer or one of the up and coming print franchises such as Prontaprint, but look at examples of their previous work first.

To produce a good leaflet design, you should consider the elements of pictures and words.

The picture should be used in a leaflet to:

- illustrate the product on offer
- emphasise points
- provide emotional stimulus
- add credibility to the story
- provide atmosphere.

The more pictures that can be used to illustrate the story, the more effective the leaflet becomes in communication terms.

The advantages of leaflets are that they do not directly compete with other matter, and that readers have comparatively more time to digest them. When planning your message you should bear these advantages in mind and make the maximum use of them.

For example, if you take a simple four-page leaflet (that is, a single folded sheet, printed on both sides) you can lead into the message with, say, a tease headline, on the front page, something to capture the readers' attention and make them curious. The next page will have illustrations and copy which will tell the story as briefly as possible and motivate the reader to seek more detailed information which you will have cleverly contrived to fill the next two pages. Then towards the end of the leaflet you will want to put a reply coupon and an action demand. This will help prompt the reader to respond.

Remember, if the leaflet is designed to be sent out to people who have asked for information, for example as the result of an advertising campaign, do not include another form requesting further information or details about how to apply on the leaflet; many organisations do make this elementary mistake.

The copy follows much the same principles as for display advertising, with the advantage that a leaflet will permit you to provide a great deal more information about the organisation than a display advertisement can carry; but care is needed here. Write the selling story, going through the stages of reasoning and argument, and conclude it with a demand for action. Then elsewhere on the leaflet (say the back page) you can provide more information that you feel will be necessary. Avoid getting readers bogged down in masses of copy, or they will lose interest and fail to respond to the message.

Produce leaflets for the task intended

Mounting a leaflet demonstration by, say, handing out large quantities in a town centre or delivery door-to-door, requires a less expensively produced leaflet than, say, one which is going to be sent out in answer to enquiries. The reasons are twofold. First, you want to use your money to the best advantage; and in order to produce a sufficient quantity for liberal distribution, you may have to sacrifice quality (in production terms). Second, the handout type of leaflet fulfils much the same job as an advertisement; that is, it puts over a message briefly and concisely. On the other hand, the leaflet you produce for people requiring further information needs to give as much relevant information as possible.

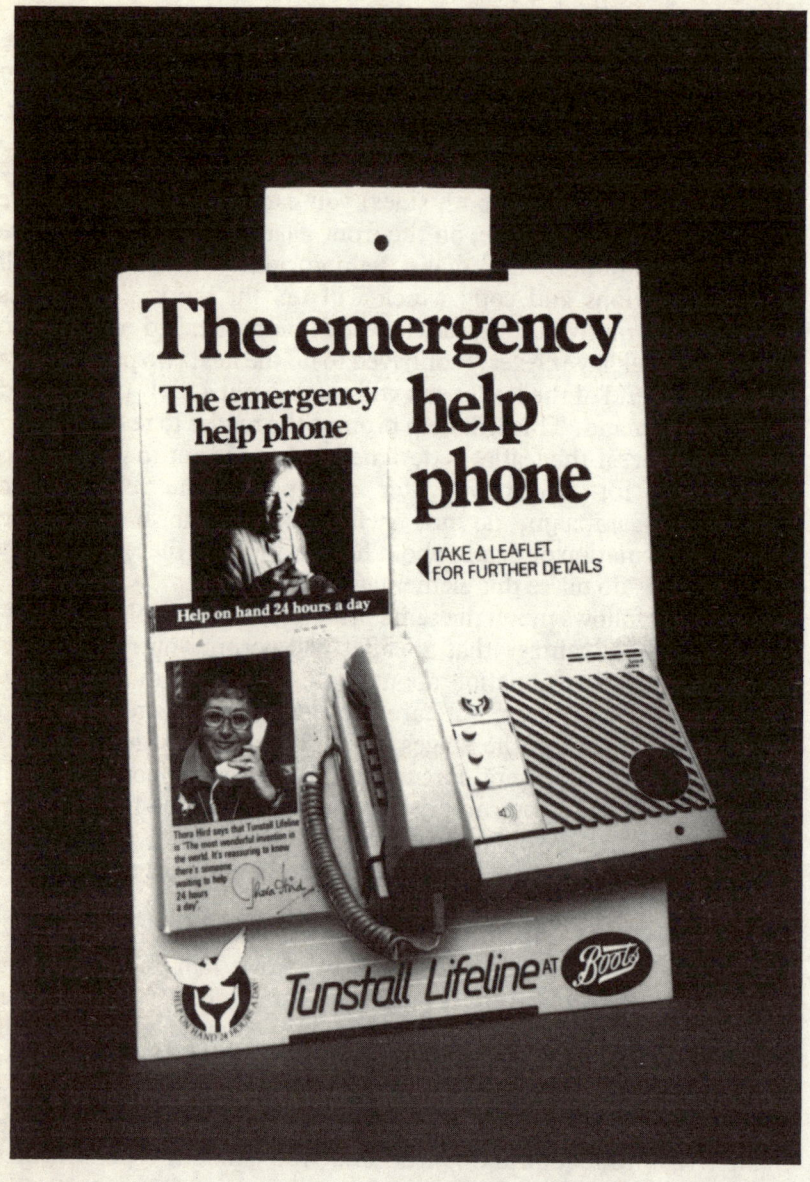

Figure 6.2 *A leaflet holder which can be either free standing or hung up. The bold headline and imaginative design make the leaflet holder very visible.* (By permission of Tunstall Telecom Ltd and Boots the Chemists Ltd)

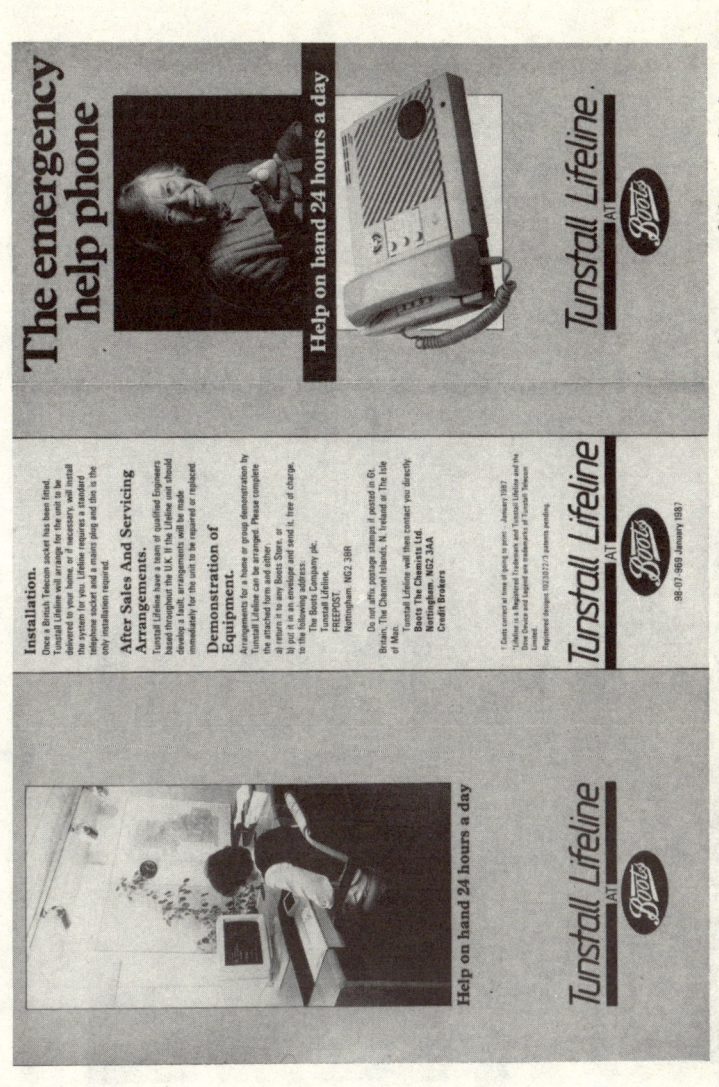

Figure 6.3 The Tunstall Lifeline at Boots leaflet shows all the ingredients of a successful exercise in communication. Printed on two sides and in full colour, it is attractively laid out and uses an effective headline to lead the reader into the body of the copy.

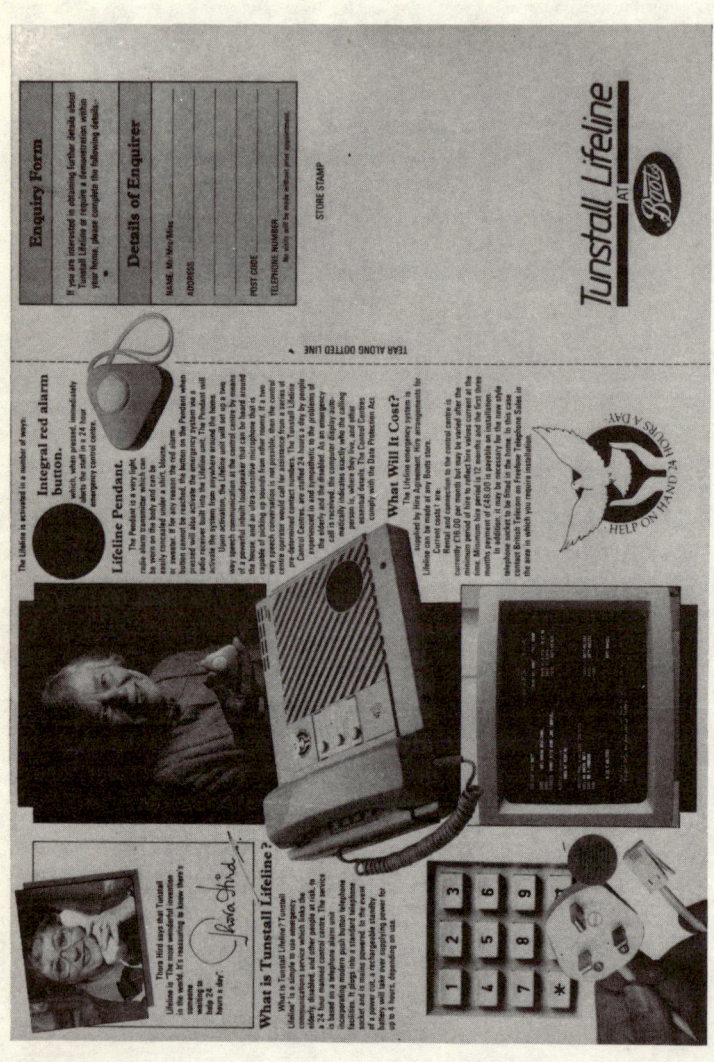

The endorsement by Thora Hird adds credibility to a novel concept. Note the amount of space allowed for the enquiry form. (By permission of Tunstall Telecom Ltd and Boots the Chemists Ltd)

In an effort to save money it is not a good idea to sacrifice design quality, but rather to print, say, a smaller, single-sided leaflet using only a single colour to produce a good, concise advertisement.

The more expensive leaflet which is required to provide more detailed information will need to have sufficient space on which to put the information (without being cramped), and a concise layout with a pleasing visual appearance is a must.

Cost elements

The key areas of cost come from the following:

Design
Artwork
Paper
Area to be printed
Number of colours
Print (on both sides/one side of paper)
Number of folds required
Printer's mark-up.

Mistakes made by the originator cannot be recovered, and the cost of several thousand leaflets, unusable because of some fundamental error, can waste a sizeable portion of the budget.

Therefore it is the originator's responsibility to check carefully that the artwork is correct and that nothing has been missed (for example, date, times, address, telephone number etc). Ask the printer for a proof and check once again that there are no errors. Even at this point, if the printer has to remake his plates or blocks because someone failed to notice a mistake on the artwork, the *originator will be charged*, but this is preferable to having to pay for a complete remake of the job.

The printer's platemaker sometimes make mistakes, and these will be seen on the proof; here again the onus is on the organisation to point them out (and to confirm in writing).

The printer will ask the originator to sign the proof as being acceptable. Again, keep a copy for reference; you cannot hold the printer liable if you should subsequently discover mistakes on the proof, but you can for his mistakes.

You do, of course, have the right to reject the finished job if it does not correspond with the proof. Here you should choose whether to accept a discount or to reject the whole job. Do not accept delivery then quibble over paying the bill.

Printing the leaflet

The local printer will advise you on the relative costs of different sizes, colour combinations and so on, and may even have the facilities to produce artwork. If there are several printers in your area it is worth getting competitive quotations, and assessing which will give best value for money. Most printers have sales representatives, and it will probably save time to telephone the companies concerned and ask the representative to call, rather than travel round from printer to printer.

Overs and unders

It is an accepted practice in the printing industry that print contracts will require you to accept a stated 'over or under' percentage (usually 5 to 10 per cent) of the quantity ordered. You will be charged for the extra quantity or given a discount for the lower. This is a necessary and generally accepted safeguard for the printer, who will do his best to produce the exact quantity; but methods devised to produce exact quantities are not generally employed.

Checking quantities

Rarely will a printer go out of his way to cheat a customer because he realises that ultimately his business will suffer if he is found out. However, errors do occur; the most common is that packages of printed matter become mislaid. On receipt it is important to check:

- that the number of packages on the delivery note tallies with those received;
- that the stated quantity of leaflets per package divides exactly into the number of packages received.

To ensure that the packages contain the required number of leaflets, the best way (other than physically to count) is to take samples of, say, 50 leaflets from several packages and weigh them. Take the average weight of the samples and use it to calculate the total per package (making an allowance for packaging) and then compare each by actually weighing them. The reason you should take several samples is because the weight of paper varies.

Looking after leaflets

Apart from the fire hazard of having large quantities of paper stacked in the front room or at the office, it is advisable to keep all those leaflets which are not required for use in their sealed packets. This not only reduces fire risk or damage from damp and dust, but also ensures that the leaflets can be kept in 'mint condition' until they are required for use. (Grubby, damaged leaflets create a bad impression.)

Storing new leaflets requires a dry, preferably low-temperature, space. This allows, at least for the first few days, a free flow of air to take away the smell of the evaporating solvents which will still be present. Remember that evaporating solvent is likely to be both inflammable and toxic if confined, so putting the leaflets in the children's bedroom or in a cupboard under the stairs is *definitely not recommended*.

Do not handle leaflets fresh from the press as the ink is likely to be still wet, and not only are they likely to smudge, but removing printers' ink from clothing or fabrics is difficult. For the same reason, do not send out leaflets which are still fresh from the printer.

Own duplicating

A number of smaller organisations duplicate their own leaflets and these can be of great value but a good layout and double-spaced typing are essential.

Direct mail – letters

Advertising by direct mail is a way of sending your message through the post to a nominated audience. In doing so, you can send a letter, a circular or a leaflet, but whatever you send must be interesting enough to prevent it being discarded before the recipient has read its contents.

Three common errors spoil the effectiveness of their direct mail advertising:

- mailing lists are out of date
- poor quality material is sent, or
- too much material (which serves to confuse the recipient).

The least expensive direct mail device is a letter. Letters have a surprising number of advantages that are not at first apparent. The letter, produced on the organisation's own headed paper, has a certain authority. It is addressed to the reader and *if it starts with his name*, he will receive it as personal correspondence. Letters are relatively inexpensive to produce and if you are only sending out a limited number, the cost is likely to be well within your budget.

The copy

As you are writing directly to the reader, the copy needs to be appropriately slanted. Write as if it were personal correspondence, and beware of giving the reader the impression that the letter is not directly written for his personal benefit.

The rules regarding sales message construction follow the principles laid down in Chapter 5, but here again, you need to reach the point of the letter as quickly as possible. An example of a very effective letter is one from Mountain Breeze, reproduced opposite. This letter was sent 'cold' to a list of business managers and received an excellent response.

Individually typed letters
The word processor provides a fantastic opportunity for individually addressed letters. For a modest outlay a machine like the IBM Action Writer can be hooked up to a personal computer to give high quality print (check with your stockist to ensure compatibility).

Duplicated letters
Duplicated letters often have a cheap appearance but are certainly less expensive than other methods and need less labour than individually typed letters. You might leave the addressee's name off the stencil or master (if photocopying) and type it on to make each letter look more personal; each letter might also be hand-signed. If it is impossible because of the sheer volume, then you can still avoid the use of the ungainly address: 'Dear Sir/Madam', by producing two stencils/masters, one addressed 'Dear Sir', the other 'Dear Madam'; or you might use another term altogether such as 'Dear Member' or 'Dear Subscriber'.

Printed letters
These provide a better impression than duplicated letters and costs can be reasonable if the organisation provides its own headed paper for the print run. If you type out the letter required with an electric typewriter (avoid rubbings out and masked mistakes), this can be used as artwork. The letters can either be hand-signed afterwards for added effect, or for large quantities, the original copy, used for artwork, can be signed.

Letters provide a useful, personal form of advertising and are of tremendous value for following up respondents to advertising or enquiries from an exhibition. They can also be used as a primary advertising or public relations medium if the target audience or public is relatively small and easily contactable through a good and up-to-date mailing list as described in Chapter 7.

Peel House, Peel Road, Skelmersdale,
Lancashire WN8 9PT Tel: 0695 21155.

Dear Executive

<u>You can actually breathe the difference a Mountain
Breeze air ioniser can make in the office</u>

You probably know already that air-conditioned offices and boardrooms with permanently closed windows often bring about feelings of stuffiness, headaches, loss of efficiency and an increase in errors.

If you've got smokers in the office then there's the problem of everybody having to share the tobacco smoke - whether they like it or not.

What may also come as a surprise to you is that the VDU screens on computers and word processors produce static which works to reduce the quality of the air.

But fortunately there is a solution to hand.

You've more than likely experienced for yourself the invigorating effect of mountain air or standing near a waterfall.

Well, a Mountain Breeze 7000 can reproduce that. It actually restores the natural balance of the air - making it cleaner and clearer.

A glance at the enclosed information will tell just how it can do this - without expensive ducting or elaborate installation.

So please don't confuse a Mountain Breeze air ioniser with conventional air cleaning systems. Mountain Breeze really does revitalise the air. Your staff will breathe the difference, and so will you.

If you have any queries - or would like a demonstration of the effectiveness of a Mountain Breeze air ioniser - then I will be glad to be of help.

Yours sincerely

Stephen R H Cross

Stephen Cross
Marketing Director

P.S. The advanced technology that makes the Mountain Breeze 7000 so markedly superior in creating cleaner, clearer air also makes it extremely cost-effective to operate.

Figure 6.4
By permission of Mountain Breeze Ltd.

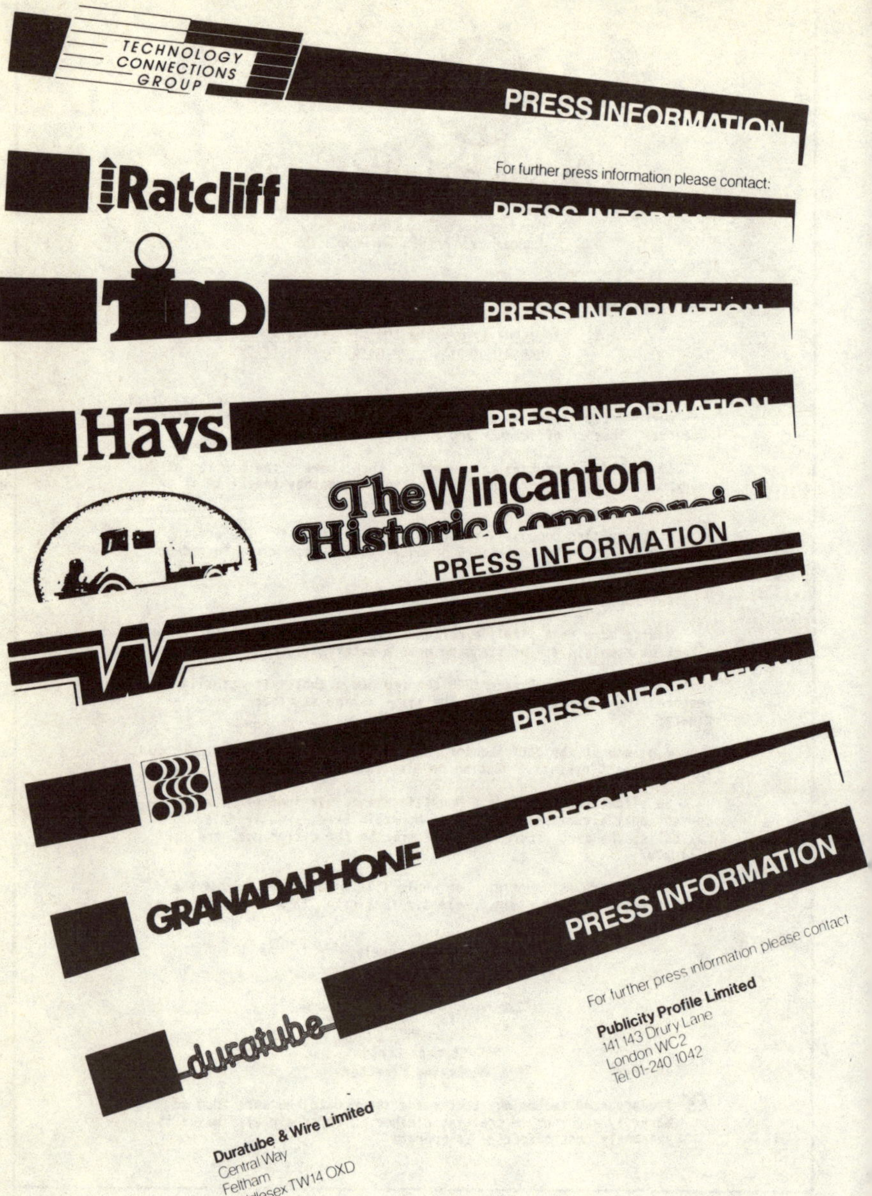
TECHNOLOGY
CONNECTIONS
GROUP
PRESS INFORMATION
Ratcliff
For further press information please contact:
Havs
The Wincanton
PRESS INFORMATION
GRANADAPHONE
PRESS INFORMATION
For further press information please contact
Publicity Profile Limited
141 143 Drury Lane
London WC2
Tel 01-240 1042
duratube
Duratube & Wire Limited
Central Way
Feltham
Middlesex TW14 OXD

Figure 6.5

CHAPTER 7
Direct Response Advertising

Direct response advertising, sometimes called 'direct marketing', is the type of advertising that seeks direct action by potential customers, ie a direct enquiry or purchase in response to the advertising. The technique is used by large and small companies. It has applications for all three types of advertising, namely consumer, trade, and business to user. One of its best advantages is that success or failure of a particular campaign can be assessed very quickly.

The simplicity and flexibility of direct response advertising, together with its relative economy, makes it an ideal vehicle for the small business. By generating leads and providing a stock of known customers it can reduce sales force costs and often reduce the number of retail and wholesale channels through which goods need to pass to reach the customer.

Direct response advertising is not just a technique, nor is it confined to specific media. Virtually any medium can be used as long as it is appropriate to the tasks being undertaken. Press, TV and mailed out leaflets are very commonly used.

Understanding the principles of direct response marketing is the key to success. Many businesses and other organisations are in one way or another involved in one of the many forms of direct response marketing but often fail to exploit it to the full.

Success requirements

Being successful means triggering a measurable direct response from the target audience. The five keys to direct marketing success are:

- The product must be high quality or the service offered unique, since other channels of distribution are unavailable or too expensive.
- The offer you make must be powerful enough to overcome inertia.
- The medium you use must be able to reach your target audience. Mailing lists that target consumers with known interests or buying histories (eg past customers) are considered to be especially effective.
- The format of the advertising must be effective and here consumer testing might make the difference between success and failure.
- Make sure the financial side is understood; know your break-even point and set limits to cut your losses.

Principles of direct response marketing

Because of the immediacy of direct response marketing activities you can measure your effectiveness by the level of response you get. It follows therefore that by constantly testing and improving your activity you can improve your results. By keeping records of all customers you deal with, you can keep going back to them as often as you like and by so doing create a dialogue with them which excludes competitors.

The two principles of direct marketing you might consider are:

- Profitable direct marketing is dependent upon building a continuing relationship between the organisation and its customers.
- Through constantly improving activities and techniques greater levels of success can be achieved.

Conflict with middlemen

Selling direct to consumers may, of course, bring the organisation into conflict with its stockists. Many retailers or middlemen refuse to stock products which they know the supplier is also attempting to sell direct to *their* customers. You may therefore be faced with a decision whether to sell your products by direct response methods *or* through normal retail channels.

Direct response marketing sequence

The sequence for direct response marketing is shown in the diagram on page 80. The most effective way of running any direct response marketing activity is based on the following steps:

- Advertise for prospective customers.
- When responses are received as a result of the advertising, ensure that the reply to the prospect is very rapid. Do not let interested prospects 'go off the boil'.
- Collect and store the names of everyone who responds to the advertising and use these names to expand your customer database.
- If the prospect replies with an order, ensure rapid supply of goods and service. This will not only prevent complaints but it will reinforce your image with the market.
- If there is no response, implement a follow-up procedure to chase up and reactivate their interest.
- Make after-sales service as important as any other activity in the recruitment of customers. Good service will reinforce people's positive attitudes to your business and will not only help you get business from them again in the future; satisfied customers are likely to recommend you to other people.
- Evaluate your success or failure in each round of the direct response market sequence. Find ways to improve your campaigns and update your offers.
- Mail out the new offer to all known customers and past prospects from your data bank. Remember that old customers, well satisfied with your products and service, are likely to be loyal.
- Start the advertising sequence again to recruit more customers.

Catalogues

Marketing through the medium of catalogues can produce very effective results. Catalogues present a challenging method of selling. Risks are high, yet once the initial period of building a market is completed successfully, catalogues may well produce more consistent sales results than any other form of direct marketing.

A catalogue is a shop. It presents an opportunity for the organisation to package its products and its image together. Catalogues, like shops in the high street, can offer either specialised or general ranges of merchandise.

People will have different expectations of products from, say, Harrods and Woolworths. Consumers behave in the same way

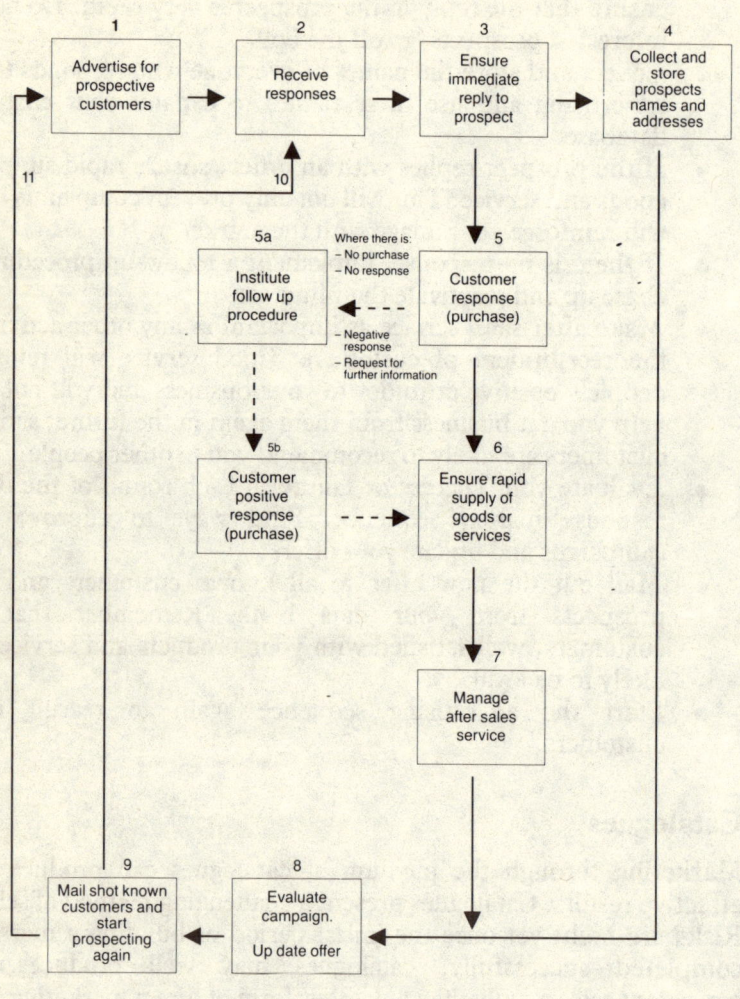

Figure 7.1

towards catalogues: image is therefore very important. A catalogue projecting a prestigious, quality impression will create a much different set of customer expectations from one featuring down-market, cut-price products. Customer expectations in terms of product range, quality and price will mirror the image a catalogue projects.

Presentation is essential
The way in which you present your catalogue is vital, therefore you will need to pay particular attention to:

- Your target audience
- The range of products offered and their prices
- The method of catalogue distribution
- The purpose of the catalogue, ie whether it is to be the principal shop window of your business or a supporting medium.

The advantages of catalogue marketing
A catalogue has a number of advantages which make it an attractive method of selling an organisation's products, namely:

- A catalogue can be sent anywhere from a single centre.
- There is no need to pay expensive sales staff where a catalogue is the principal method of selling.
- Where a catalogue is used as a supporting medium, it may be sent out to reduce sales force call frequency to regular customers or to cover smaller customers, upon whom it might otherwise be uneconomic to call.
- Investment in costly retail sites and shopfittings is avoided.
- Experience suggests that once the business is established, revenue will be more predictable than through any other form of direct marketing.

Benefits to the customer

- Customers can shop in the comfort of their own home, at a time which suits them. There are no parking problems, no carrying heavy packages or the embarrassment of having to wait while a sales clerk checks the worthiness of their credit card!
- Catalogues are often used by customers to give them ideas about what to buy.

- Customers can use a catalogue to compare and evaluate competitive brands, prices and features.
- Catalogues are often kept for reference, particularly those concerned with specialist products such as books, briefcases, office furniture, camera equipment, car accessories, DIY products, tools, paints and industrial protective clothing.
- Catalogue companies often offer good facilities for credit and many customers buy through catalogues because of relatively easy repayment methods offered.

Risks and dangers of catalogue marketing

For all its advantages, a catalogue is a high risk medium where it is used as the principal shop window of the business. The reasons for this are:

- Catalogues demand highly creative inputs, which involve expensive, professional services, eg photographers, graphic artists, copywriters etc.
- Catalogues are very expensive to produce.
- Costs of inventory and service support systems must be borne before the first catalogue is sent out to a potential customer – hence a high financial risk.
- Very high reliance has to be placed on creative presentation. If the creative elements do not work, the success of a new catalogue is considerably endangered.
- The lead times are often long. It takes time to assemble an inventory, plan layout, complete photography, proof, print and despatch a catalogue. Long lead times present the risks of fashions changing, prices changing or competitors stealing a march.

Making your catalogue successful

The secret of a successful catalogue is based on building up repeat sales from existing customers. You therefore need to ensure that you hold and retain the loyalty of each new customer through offering good merchandise which is well-presented, and by providing a high standard of customer service and complaint-handling procedures, as well as keeping in touch with the needs of your customers to exploit the opportunity to the full.

There are three phases of business development, which you should think about:

Recruitment. First you must recruit sufficient customers to pay for your initial investment and provide enough revenue to continue to expand. Initial distribution of your catalogue will need to be worked out. You could advertise your catalogue, send out your mailings, distribute catalogues directly to existing or known potential customers or insert copies in a popular publication. Methods of obtaining mailing lists and using advertising and so forth are discussed elsewhere in this chapter.

Building business through existing customers is the next phase. Experience suggests that upwards of three-quarters of a successful, established catalogue's business will come from regular customers. You must therefore work on these to:

- Persuade customers to purchase with increasing frequency, through promotional inducements, discounts, cross-selling techniques and by ensuring that your range and prices meet your customers' requirements.
- Maintain customer loyalty through good customer service and complaint-handling procedures.
- Keep in touch with your customers by keeping records of their purchases, ensuring that you note changes of address.
- Encourage existing customers to promote your business to their friends, colleagues and acquaintances. Again, good service, good products and prices, together with inducements, will aid this activity considerably. Furthermore, in encouraging customers to promote your catalogue you will reinforce their loyalty and commitment to your business.

In this second phase the need for developing a knowledge of your customers and their purchasing trends is axiomatic.

Many successful catalogues provide coded order forms as a means of collecting data. Such data can be stored on computer for cross-referencing. You might also consider setting up a panel of customers from among your regulars to test new catalogues, solicit merchandise ideas, assess your service quality and so on. Professional advice on the panel composition will almost certainly be necessary to ensure that data obtained is valid.

Expansion of your business is logically the third phase of your building process. Here you are concerned with:

- Using the economics of your print runs to distribute more copies of your catalogue to potential customers. Once your origination costs are covered by your regular customers, the

costs of distributing more copies will be relatively inexpensive.
- Experiment with your inventory to improve order value. Once you have a predictable business level you can afford to test ideas for new products.
- Increase the sophistication of your customer information through professionally executed market research and image studies. Use this knowledge to focus more precisely on aspects of your catalogue that will make it more effective.

Cross-selling

Customers who have bought and tried one of your products and been satisfied by it are likely to be good prospects for other products in your range. A very successful technique is to follow up each customer with a personalised mailing for another product, the satisfaction gained from the first purchase endorsing the new offer. Do not therefore discard addresses of customers. It's a lot less expensive directing mail offers to known customers than to have to trawl for new ones. You can also use your mailing list of known customers to pre-test your new products or services.

You will probably find that a combination of buying initial lists and building your own from known customers will be the most effective in terms of sales and economy.

To use mailing lists, particularly those which are paid for, it's a good idea to run a few tests with one or two thousand addresses initially. One way to reduce the number of 'gone aways' on your mailing lists is to ensure that your name and address appear on the envelope so that you receive back all returned mail. Use the returned mail to correct your lists.

Getting the message to the customer

The most precise, accurate and direct method of getting a message to the customer is to use the post. The Post Office runs deals for major customers including a 'free posting' offer and substantial discounts especially for first-time users. A list of Post Office services appears on page 94.

To use the mail, however, accurate mailing lists are required and there are basically three ways to obtain lists:

- Construct your own from local directories, from Yellow Pages and so forth; this method involves a lot of time.
- Buy or rent a list from a list broker which will cost you from £40 to £60 per 1000 addresses.
- Collect names of existing customers from, say, past

campaigns, replies to competitions, or simply compile the names of people who fill in your guarantee cards.

You should strive for the last method because the list is compiled from your own customers and they will have a greater propensity to buy from you again than people taken cold from any other mailing list.

Door-to-door deliveries (business and consumer)

For just over £30 per 1000 (less for large quantities) the Post Office will distribute your literature to either households or businesses in prescribed areas. While you cannot aim it towards a named person, you can designate the job title on the envelope, Managing Director, Office Manager etc. Contact your local Postal Services representative for further information.

Insertions into magazines reaching your market

- Specific trade magazines charge on average £50–£60 per 1000 for inserts, either loose or bound-in.
- General business magazines, which are often produced regionally, cost from £35 to £75 per 1000. Local business magazines reach a specific geographical area and to expand beyond a particular area you may need several such magazines.
- National consumer magazines or colour supplements attached to the national press take inserts and will also regionalise (but usually cover very wide geographic areas). The cost is reasonable, usually from £16 to £20 per 1000.

Guarantees

If you give a guarantee follow the addressee with a personalised letter or a new offer. Once again, do not waste addresses; they provide a vital link with known customers.

Integration into the sales attack

Regardless of how high the response may be in a direct response campaign, its value can very easily be dissipated. It's all too easy to lose sight of the campaign objective – sales.

When a campaign is run correctly the right sort of arrangements will have been made to deal with a high response. A campaign that is overwhelmed by response and for which there is an inadequate ability to cope with enquiries will lead to wasted opportunities and loss of prestige.

The success of any direct response campaign really has to be measured in terms of what sales it is achieving rather than merely the number of enquiries.

The key elements of integrating the campaign into the sales attack are to:

- Ensure a good organisation is in place for the following up of enquiries quickly and efficiently
- Make sales visits to prospects before they lose their enthusiasm; the longer the delay the greater the risk will be that the prospect will be lost.

Marketing Week gives us a good example of failure due to poor organisation:

> A well known agricultural chemicals company wished to promote a specialist product to a relatively small audience on behalf of one of its major distributors. As the market could be carefully defined, direct mail was the obvious choice and produced a response rate of 18 per cent, which delighted both the manufacturer and the distributor, who was to handle the response.
>
> The high level of response presented a perfect opportunity for the distributor's sales team to capitalise on a clearly demonstrated interest in what was an effective specialist market.
>
> But, despite the fact that the offer items – useful technical guides – were in stock, it was weeks, not days before they were mailed to the respondents. And internal disputes over how the sales leads should be handled meant that replies never reached the sales force.
>
> Thousands of pounds of potential business were lost, because the manufacturer and distributor had failed to make preparation for dealing with the response.
>
> To make sure that this does not happen companies running direct-response campaigns should start planning early.

The management of replies needs to be clearly thought out and *Marketing Week* suggests that guidelines be laid down on how replies are to be processed and staff well prepared to handle procedures. In the enthusiasm to mount a campaign sufficient funds need to be put on one side from the budget to meet the costs realistically. A campaign can always be mounted progressively, ie a region or an area at a time, so that facilities match response.

Again *Marketing Week* suggests that:

The key is to keep it simple. A complicated time-consuming procedure may be intellectually pleasing, but it can slow down processing and lead to an unmanageable backlog – resulting in frayed tempers and a loss of impetus.

Enquiries must be sent as quickly as possible to the people who will follow them up – either the company's own salesmen or those of a distributor.

The Automobile Association, for instance, recognises the cost benefits of immediate action and spares no effort in following up leads. Within hours of receiving replies to mailings promoting company membership, basic information is telexed to local sales offices and the actual reply card or coupon is sent by Datapost overnight, to provide full details. Potentially large account leads are telephoned to the relevant sales office for immediate attention.

The psychological effect on the prospect is heightened if the salesman is able to produce the original enquiry, whether it is a coupon or a reply card.

The sales staff should be highly motivated to follow leads quickly and efficiently. To make the most cost-effective use of selling time it is important to try to keep sales staff to their normal call cycles but the danger of a prospect going cold is real. To overcome this *Marketing Week* suggest that a bounce-back letter be sent thanking the enquirer and advising that the relevant offer demonstration etc will be undertaken by his local representative. *Marketing Week* also suggest that the salesman's name and telephone number be given, should the enquirer wish to make contact.

Such letters will add more to the cost of the campaign but experience has shown that the extra expense is almost always outweighed by the goodwill generated and by the fact that the respondent's interest is maintained.

Marketing Week also suggests ways of dealing with prospects who do not buy, for no matter how good the campaign some prospects may doubt the product or be too busy or too lazy to go to the next step in the negotiation. The skilful use of telephone selling techniques is recommended to turn prospects into customers.

However, a word of warning: skill is required and often businesses do not have skilled telephone sales people. Telemarketing companies (companies which specialise in telephone selling) can be used and these people make their money by being successful. However, good selection and briefing are essential in the use of telemarketing companies.

For any small businessman and his sales staff, ability to sell on the telephone successfully, is important and for a relatively small sum training courses can be obtained.

Credit cards
You will gain more business if you make it easier for people to pay. By providing a credit card facility you are in effect offering credit financed by the purchaser. For the few per cent it costs it is well worth providing the facility.

Supporting the direct response advertising campaign
The integration of campaign and sales force objectives is essential and even more can be achieved with the support of additional publicity. Obviously with an interesting product and story, PR opportunities will arise and this will add credibility to the product, for reasons given in Chapter 3.

For a lot of products sold through direct marketing methods the consumer rarely has a chance to see them other than as photographs, so there is much to be said for trying to find ways of letting people see them in reality. A number of opportunities can be created through exhibitions and displays. For example, one double glazing company I know hires space in a shopping centre.

Follow-up service
As we said at the beginning of this chapter, it will often be easier to solicit new orders from past customers than from cold prospects. Service, to ensure the customer is constantly happy with the product, is an important ingredient.

Not all small businessmen have the time, but remember that the end of the transaction does not usually mean the end of customers' satisfaction. Keep the customer happy for repeat sales and remember that every enchanted customer generates free publicity.

Mail order schemes for protecting the consumer buying through cash-off-the-page advertisements

Publications have both a moral and commercial interest in ensuring that their readers are not cheated or let down by their advertisers. In order to protect the interests of readers and limit their own liability to claims a number of schemes have been set up by publishers' associations. The aims of these schemes are to provide reassurance to their members' readers that advertisements soliciting cash with order (cash-off-the-page), are genuine offers and that readers will be reimbursed for losses they incur should the advertiser default in sending or replacing faulty goods sent in response to an advertisement contained in the pages of their publications.

There are a number of schemes and all have common elements. Purchasers have cover when they buy 'cash with order' from any publication which is a member of one of the following:

> Newspaper Publishers' Association – dealing with national daily newspapers
> Periodical Publishers' Association Limited—dealing with magazines
> The Newspaper Society – dealing with regional and local newspapers
> Scottish Newspaper Proprietors' Association – dealing with Scottish regional and local newspapers
> The Scottish Daily Newspaper Society – dealing with Scottish daily newspapers.

Any newspaper or magazine involved in a mail protection scheme will publicise this fact through the printing of short statements to this effect. Such information will be headed 'Dealers' Protection Scheme' or 'Mail Order Protection Scheme'.

MOPS

The National Newspaper Mail Order Protection Scheme – MOPS – is the largest of the schemes designed to protect mail order purchases. It covers members of the National Newspaper Association Ltd as listed on page 90.

To enable postal shoppers to have complete confidence when placing their orders, MOPS was set up in 1975 in consultation with the Office of Fair Trading and under an agreement between the national newspapers, the Institute of Practitioners in Advertising and the Incorporated Society of British Advertisers. Its function is to reimburse readers who might otherwise lose money if the goods which have been ordered fail to be delivered as a result of an advertiser going into liquidation or bankruptcy, or ceasing to trade. It also covers readers who have returned goods and not received a refund from a failed advertiser.

The administrators of the scheme also protect the public by demanding a formal application from each new mail order advertiser. This ensures that the applicant is in every way suitable before the administrators recommend that their advertising is accepted. Even then, it does not automatically follow that the advertising will be

Associated Newspapers Group Ltd
Daily Mail
Mail on Sunday
Weekend Magazine
YOU/Colour Magazine

Express Newspapers Ltd
Daily Express
Sunday Express
Sunday Express Magazine
Daily Star
Evening Standard

The Daily Telegraph Ltd
The Daily Telegraph
The Sunday Telegraph
The Telegraph Sunday Magazine

The Financial Times Ltd
The Financial Times

The Guardian & Manchester Evening News Ltd
The Guardian

Mirror Group Newspapers Ltd
Daily Mirror
Sunday Mirror
The Sunday People
Daily Record
Sunday Mail

News Group Newspapers Ltd
News of the World
The Sun
Sunday (Colour Magazine)

Newspaper Publishing Plc
The Independent

The Observer Ltd
The Observer
The Observer Colour Magazine

Times Newspapers Ltd
The Times
The Sunday Times
The Sunday Times Colour Magazine

published as the final decision rests with the national newspaper concerned.

In practice, the scheme has been extraordinarily successful in protecting readers' interests and, in relation to the number of transactions concluded by post, claims for compensation have been negligible.

The scope of the scheme
The central fund of the scheme protects a reader if the advertisement:

(a) is inserted in a national newspaper
(b) describes a product giving details of the price and the address from which it may be obtained
(c) directly asks readers to order the product by post by sending a remittance with the order.

There is also the overriding condition that the advertiser must have been recommended for acceptance into the scheme and, to show this, approved advertisements will, in many cases, include the MOPS symbol in their layout, or the initials MOPS in the bottom left-hand corner of the advertisement.

Where an advertisement has been inserted without MOPS'

recommendation, readers' losses are the sole responsibility of the newspaper concerned. Thus the sight of the MOPS symbol in an advertisement is an assurance of consumer protection.

Application for membership
Organisations wishing to become members of MOPS must make a formal application to the scheme's Management Committee. Forms are available from any member newspaper or from the scheme's own offices.

> The National Newspapers Mail Order Protection Scheme Ltd
> 16 Tooks Court
> London EC4A 1LB
> telephone 01-405 6806/9.

There are five application forms, namely:
Form 1. The principal form which asks for information about the advertiser to establish its status as a *bona fide* business.
Form 2 requires information about the merchandise to be advertised and should be accompanied by a draft of the advertisement. The committee may request samples of goods being advertised.
Form 3 is the contract between the advertiser and the scheme. The contract requires the advertiser to conform to all current legislation and the British Code of Advertising Practice.
Forms 4/4a are only required to be submitted if an advertising agency is employed. These forms require information about the agency and require its membership to the scheme on an advertiser by advertiser basis.
Form 6 is the formal contract between the advertiser and the individual member newspapers and is filed centrally by the scheme's secretariat.

Each applicant is required to send its audited accounts and balance sheet together with the application forms. Failure to do so will inevitably delay the application process. For *newly established businesses* where there are no audited accounts, current management accounts or an opening financial statement should be sent with the application.

MOPS will, upon receipt of an application, seek a credit survey through a reputable credit reporting organisation. This will normally take about a month to complete. The application is then placed before the scheme's Management Committee for consideration. The Committee meets weekly and results are notified immediately through the advertiser's advertising agency if there is one or to the applicant direct where there is not.

Fees
The appropriate fee must accompany the application forms. Fees are set out annually between April and March for each ensuing year. Fees are based on a scale which is calculated against the amount of advertising expenditure the applicant proposes to spend. The current scale of fees is always sent to applicants along with application forms.

Fees are not refundable and may not be carried over from one year to the next without the consent of the scheme's Management Committee. Consent will only be given where advertising expenditure has fallen short of the amount of fee paid in the year. To apply for fees to be carried over a written request is necessary.

If an applicant is not accepted by the scheme the fee is refunded in full.

If after making an initial application to the scheme an advertiser spends more on advertising than was proposed on the application forms, additional fees must be paid. MOPS monitors members' advertising very closely and will not hesitate to contact advertisers if they do not send additional fees for the additional advertising placed.

Exemptions from the scheme
The following categories of advertising are currently exempted from the scheme and no application for membership is required in respect thereof:

(a) the sale of perishable foodstuffs
(b) any product which appeals to fear or superstition, eg lucky charms, horoscopes etc
(c) those asking readers to send for catalogues, brochures or details of products, which are supplied free or for a charge of £1 or less. Subsequent sales from such catalogues, brochures etc which are inserted with goods ordered in response to mail order advertising are also not protected by the scheme.
(d) those advertisements inviting readers to visit retail premises
(e) those which offer a 'service', such as membership of clubs, magazine subscriptions, theatre tickets, film processing etc. However, in the case of film processing, if the advertiser offers a replacement film to be purchased in addition to the charge for processing, then readers are protected for the cost of the replacement film, but not the processing

(f) advertisements inviting readers to purchase goods for 25 pence or less
(g) those which offer goods on a self-liquidating or other premium basis, eg where readers have to send, in addition to cash, some proof of product purchase, such as a label, stamps etc from products obtained through retail outlets
(h) advertisements which appear under a newspaper's own classified heading or in classified columns such as 'PERSONAL', 'MOTORING', 'HOUSE & GARDEN', etc
(i) those appearing under a 'GARDENING' classification heading which offer trees, shrubs, plants and other growing things, chemicals and fertilisers. The scheme, however, protects readers where the products are 'hardware' products, eg greenhouses, tools etc
(j) those which offer goods on approval or on a 'cash on delivery' basis, or where the reader is required to send only a small sum to cover carriage or postage costs only
(k) medical products, eg patent medicines.
(From MOPS covering letter to applicants to the scheme.)

Use of logo

When an advertiser's application is approved by the Management Committee the advertiser will be permitted to include the logo MOPS in *cash-off-the-page* advertisements covered by the scheme, and in *member publications only*, to indicate membership of the scheme. It is not permissible to use any form of wording to accompany the logo, such as 'readers are fully protected since we are members of the Mail Order Protection Scheme' etc.

The logo *must not* however be used in any of the following circumstances:

- Where the advertisement is not 'cash-off-the page'
- In classified advertisements
- In publications which are not members of the scheme
- In the literature mailed out by the advertiser
- On the headed note paper of the advertiser.

A number of advertisers have been prosecuted under the Trade Descriptions Act for using MOPS logo incorrectly.

Compliance with MOPS regulations is therefore very important and advice should be sought from the scheme's secretariat for any query regarding the legitimacy of the use of the MOPS logo.

Royal Mail services

The Royal Mail offer a variety of services and discounts to direct mail advertisers.

The main service has two major functions for the direct mail advertiser – getting the sales message to the customer and then handling the response. The following list of services is offered by the Royal Mail:

- *Bulk Rebates Service* is offered to postal customers mailing more than 4250 second class letters all pre-sorted into post towns and counties. Sliding scale discounts are offered from 15 to 30 per cent, mail being delivered within seven days.
- *First Class Letter Contracts* for pre-sorted mail offer a discount of up to 12 per cent, mail being delivered the next day.
- *Second Class Discount* for pre-sorted mail offers discounts with mail being delivered within three days.
- *Incentive Discounts for Growth* are offered to larger mailers spending more than £20,000 per year.
- *The Direct Mail Deposit System* allows direct mailers to protect themselves from sudden postage price increases for up to six months in advance. For a minimum of 5000 identical items the mailing price is served by a deposit equivalent to 25 per cent of the postage cost.
- *Introductory offer* for first time users for a mail shot of up to 1000 items qualifies for free postage – or for a larger first shot, a contribution towards postage. This could be as much as 40 per cent plus whatever discounts have already been taken.
- *Household Delivery Service* is the Post Office's door-to-door distribution service. It offers delivery of unaddressed promotional material to domestic addresses in whatever size of area the customer chooses.
- *Methods of Stamping* including franking machines and printed postage impressions (for more than 5000 letters at a time through a nominated post office).
- *Business Reply* paid cards or envelopes are printed to Post Office specifications and can be included in both direct mail shots and household delivery items.
- *Freepost* is used where respondents cannot be provided with reply cards or envelopes. By quoting the freepost advertising customers reply at the advertiser's expense. There is a small licence fee plus 0.5p on each reply received as a charge.

CHAPTER 8
Making News

Anyone who waits for headline-making news to happen is unlikely to succeed in creating interest in his organisation. Not all news makes a lead story but this is not to say that material published in the rest of the paper is not read; otherwise proprietors would not bother to produce papers the size they are. Within the confines of good sense and responsibility an active publicity seeker will try to have something published every week, even if it is only in the local papers.

News stories

In finding material for news stories, there are the ongoing activities of the organisation – these will appeal to the media:

- product/promotional news
- special conferences
- staff outings
- special activities
- personality stories
- sponsorship
- sports activities.

Product/Promotional news

News featuring products is very valuable in that it brings the product name in front of the reader, helping to reinforce the reader's memory of the product and its name. The use of trade magazines and news sheets to publicise product innovations, new applications, new models, new sizes, new packaging, new promotions etc is extremely valuable in bringing the company and product name to the reader's notice. These are simply handled by a press release and photo.

Everything newsworthy about the business's products should be despatched to the trade press. In generating news for the consumer media obviously more sophisticated stories will be required. A new invention can be described as a technical or application breakthrough. A new model can be publicised by inviting the press to an unveiling ceremony. A promotional campaign might get a mention or two if handled well.

Special conferences

Special conferences organised by the business to discuss topics of interest, eg health and safety, can be of benefit in two ways. First from the interest generated by participants, and second from the media coverage. Ideally, controversial or innovative subjects can be used to call users or opinion formers to a meeting. An agricultural distributor might call a meeting of farmers to discuss, say, use of fertiliser or new Common Market regulations. The trick is to find someone of eminence to chair the meeting. Treat the publicity side by press releases or by inviting the press.

Staff outings

Outings should, by and large, be reported light-heartedly, unless they have a deeper significance than just a pleasure trip. They are best treated as a picture and one paragraph caption. Material may interest the local press and sometimes the trade press.

Special activities

Demonstrations, stunts, exhibitions and so forth provide ample opportunities for photo calls and photo caption releases. The visit of the local beauty queen will get the local press, the visit of Miss UK may hit the nationals.

The linking of events with personalities can often turn a small event into a newsworthy one. Inviting fairly minor celebrities from, say, *The Archers* can often create just as much publicity as a major personality.

Personality stories

In maintaining the frequency of a public relations campaign, personality stories are invaluable, especially for the local press, as they are not only of local interest but provide a human angle to the aims of the organisation. They can be used to help.

1. establish a new chairman, local sales manager etc
2. widen coverage of interest in the organisation

3. attract people with special interests
4. create an image for the organisation.

The newly elected chairman, who may have to win the support of the local community, can be greatly assisted by a 'pen portrait' in the local paper. The story should include sufficient biographical information to be relevant to local interest. A statement from him of the aims of the organisation, and his ideas on how he will help achieve them, will probably be published at this stage of his career, whereas this may be considered tendentious later.

Beware, however, that the public relations operations of the organisation are not turned to promoting the man. Very often a new chairman, having a taste for publicity, turns the whole publicity machinery to getting himself mentioned in the 'paper'. The chairman is, after all, the figurehead of the organisation and stories about him should be used to project the aims of the organisation.

Promoting the figureheads helps to create confidence in the business among customers, financial institutions and those useful to the business, by showing that the organisation is well led.

Sponsorship

Sponsorship is a growing source of funds for voluntary organisations, sports institutions and for things like racing cars, sail boards and expeditions to Outer Mongolia. The benefit to the business is publicity and, to those being sponsored, funds. New tax concessions for charitable gifts may cover many aspects of sponsorship such as local theatre and sport. Sponsorship projects need to be carefully planned in order to ensure that the maximum publicity falls on the business.

Sports activities

Some companies, particularly those with younger employees, have successful football, tennis, netball or rugby teams etc; and local press coverage of their activities can be a useful way both of creating a healthy image and of gaining the attention of sports enthusiasts. Team games with suppliers or customers may not only bring relationships closer but may also provide something interesting for local and trade press.

Other ways of projecting the organisation

Local press visits

The feature writer from the local press can and should be invited to see activities of the organisation. The way of approaching him can either be directly on the telephone (which is best) or by letter via the editor.

Once he has agreed to come, produce a simple set of notes about the organisation. (These are not necessarily intended for publication, but as an aid.) They should be logical and brief, with each paragraph under an easy reference heading:

1. History of the organisation
2. Aims of the organisation
3. Recent achievements
4. Details of activities happening during the visit.

These notes, probably not exceeding 500 words, should, if only for the sake of professionalism, be neatly typed and presented in a folder along with some interesting photographs. The writer will then have sufficient background material on which to base his story.

Further assistance can be given to the feature writer by checking out where the paper's key circulation areas are, and then ensuring that members of the organisation who live in these areas are available for interview. This not only suits the paper, but will also ensure that the feature article creates the maximum amount of local interest when it appears.

You or the chairman should be on hand to make a comment. It is a fact of life that so many chairmen do 'open their mouth and put their foot in it'. In their enthusiasm they are apt to say too much or are so wrapped up in hearing themselves speak that they wander into irrelevance.

Press receptions

Small or local organisations are advised not to run lavish receptions for the press. Not only are they unnecessary, but they can waste funds that might well be better used on other publicity projects. However, a simple wine and cheese party or inexpensive buffet for the press, say for the opening of new premises or for launching a major campaign, might well be of value, if only to bring as many press people as possible together.

Running a press reception calls for good organisation and skill and it should be remembered that the attending press have to get there, so choose a central venue with clear directions and address. It might even be necessary to provide transport from a central point to take them to the reception, if it is at all difficult to find.

Let the press know in time; this is where so many organisations fall down. From experience, it should be no sooner than three weeks and no later than ten days before the event takes place. Any earlier and dates saved are taken up by other matters, and any later it may be too late, as most reporters have fairly full diaries.

As with other press operations, adequate notes must be available for reporters and journalists to take away.

If, for some reason, it is necessary to cancel the reception, not only is it essential to write a polite letter of apology but, if there is any fear at all that those invited might not have had time to receive the letters, telephone them. A little effort can save a great amount of time and help maintain good relations with the press.

Press reception checklist
The checklist below might be useful for planning a good reception.

Venue
  Location. Is it central or will you need to send transport to pick up the press?
  For how many will transport be required?
  Is it convenient for press people?
  Are maps, directions and road signs necessary?
  Date
  Time. Will it fit in with public transport?

Venue facilities
  Is a bar available?
  Is it necessary to provide outside caterers?
  Are seating facilities adequate?
  Are there ladies' and gentlemen's toilets?
  Is a public address system required?
  Are telephones available?
  Is there adequate heating/ventilation?
  Indoors or outdoors? (Latest weather forecast if the latter.)

Food and drink
  For predominantly male or predominantly female guests?
  Will it serve to replace lunch or dinner, or will it merely be a snack?
  How long are guests likely to stay?
  Buffet or sit-down?
  Cost per head?
  Money available?

Are there sufficient people to run the catering? (Even outside caterers often do not bring along enough people to run catering adequately.)
Ensure waiters or waitresses are of pleasant disposition.

Invitations
   Print correctly. Name of organisation, address for RSVP, venue, date, time, dress.
   Despatch. First-class mail; 21 days in advance of event.
   Confirmation. Replies received. Telephone check to non-replies. Maps, directions etc sent out (if not already sent with the invitation).
   Publicity. Issue name badges for everyone. Have folders of notes and photographs available for everyone to take away with them. Prepared speech of presentation not exceeding 20 minutes by organisation chairman. A photographer to cover the reception.

Gaining countrywide publicity

Not all small businesses need national publicity because their market catchment is purely local. Yet a national news item mentioning even a very local company may help to increase local awareness of the business and gain a greater number of customers. Obviously an organisation with a national coverage of business will need to find ways of generating countrywide publicity.

There are several key media through which a publicity campaign may gain broad coverage and on which a national campaign can be built:

National
Press: newspapers, magazines, television papers etc. *Television*: BBC is national and so is Network IBA. *Radio*: Radio One, Two and Three are national and so is Network Radio Four.

Regional
Regional television
Granada, Thames, Central etc cover regions but a PR operation reaching all IBA stations will make up national coverage.

Local radio
BBC or IBA do not cover such wide areas as the television regions, but coverage of them all will create almost national exposure.

Regional papers
Either evening, daily or Sunday, can be used together to reach an almost national readership.

Trade press
Most service and trade industries have a press, which goes to people participating in each particular trade sector. Publications are usually national and some are international and can be used to reach potential customers and opinion formers.

The organisation's news has to compete with national disasters, business news, scandals and, of course, news from other organisations and so starting a national campaign is no easy matter.

Anyone embarking on such a project is likely to suffer a great deal of disappointment before he sees his first material published.

How to generate national publicity

Let us now look at a few ideas that will help generate publicity on a national scale.

The news release service is probably the base from which to start. Include the national papers, women's magazines, television and radio editors on the mailing list. Send them only stories which will appeal to national audiences of specific groups (women, children, animal-lovers, car-owners). If the advice given concerning news releases in Chapter 9 is taken, then it should not be long before odd pieces start appearing.

A feature article in the press
The way to approach a publication is to write to the editor. Choose one you feel will most likely be sympathetic, provided of course the story will interest their readers. However, it is necessary to sell the idea to the editor and, in doing so, it is a good idea to suggest the angle of the story and how it is likely to appeal to the readers, for example:

Emotional
Animal welfare, children, the sick.

Public good
Helping aged, helping refugees, fighting pollution.

Special interest
Bagpipe collecting, flying, parachuting.

Expertise
Write articles around the subject of the business, for example 'How to benefit from life assurance', 'Woodworm', 'Cottage renovation'. Create the image of an expert. If nothing else, it will give you credibility in your customers' eyes.

In order to have a story published it is essential that you select suitable publications and then study them to get a feel for the editorial style. Produce an outline of your story, collect together some interesting illustrations and then contact your selected publications and offer them your ideas for an article.

Unless you can write to the standard required by national publications, it is not advised that you actually write the article (as it may well be returned because its literary execution is not acceptable, rather than because of the theme of the article). It may be possible to persuade a local journalist who is sympathetic to the organisation to write an article for a small fee.

Radio and television

There can be no warmer feeling for an organisation than the thrill of getting something on radio or television. There are absolutely hundreds of opportunities with four television channels, four national radio channels and local radio stations mushrooming in every large conurbation. Yet many organisations tend to shy away from the mass broadcasting media. The reasons for this are not clear, but it may be through lack of information (not knowing who to write to), or a feeling that they are not important enough to get on television. The rest of this chapter, then, is devoted to getting the organisation into the mass broadcasting media. Let us look at some of the programmes that might be offered material.

News programmes
Both radio and television run news programmes as a service to their listeners and viewers. These can vary from five minutes to an hour. Obviously, the shorter the programme the more it will be concerned with sensational news; and unless the organisation happens to be making the headlines it is unlikely to be featured. The exception might be a very funny story, which could be used to end the programme.

The longer programmes, such as *Today* or *The World at One*, may use material, particularly if it is controversial, has a certain amount of public goodwill, has some novelty value or something which will appeal to special interest groups, say musicians or motorists. The news-release service should be extended to include the news editors of the longer programmes.

Talk-back programmes (phone-in)
The BBC and IBA began using talk-back as a way of gaining audience participation in the 1970s. There are basically two types of talk-back programmes.

First, there is the type which invites members of the general public to telephone in, to put a question to a leading personality. Second, there are those such as the *Jimmy Young Show*, during which the presenter will telephone somebody who has written in – for a chat! In the former, the whole programme is devoted to phoned-in questions, and in the latter, only a fraction of the show is taken up by 'the chat'.

Chat shows
The editors of chat shows, especially on local radio, will invite local businessmen or interesting people connected with business to take part in chat programmes. Such programmes give you the opportunity to project both your company and yourself. Some tips are given later in this chapter.

Children's programmes
The children's television programmes are an ideal way of gaining support, if something from the organisation can be included. One of the best examples of this happened a few years back, when the RNLI had an item on *Blue Peter*, only a day or two before a national flag day.

By and large the editors of children's programmes tend to choose material which is either educational, of public goodwill, scientific, involves travel or is concerned with animals, and which is not politically or religiously biased. Therefore some organisations with such interests can probably provide ideas to the editors. Again watch the programmes to help you plan an idea.

Current affairs programmes
These are constantly on the look-out for new material to fill their programmes and the organisation might get an interview or even a film feature. Such programmes as *Panorama* and *This Week*, are particularly useful and the adventurous publicity seeker should watch them to see how they are presented and to get ideas on how to present material to them. Probably the best way of approaching them is to:

1. Write a short letter to the editor or producer of the selected programme suggesting that an item on the organisation might be included. Say why you feel it concerns his listeners and suggest how it might be treated – film, interview etc. (But be realistic.)
2. Include a short set of background notes (as you would for a magazine article).
3. Recent photographs, to give the editor the flavour of the organisation's activities, should be included.
4. Also include recent brochures, leaflets and so forth.
5. Put them all in a loose-leaf binder, which bears the name and address of the organisation (use a gummed label).

One further point: if you wish it to be passed around to other editors, say so in the letter, otherwise an editor rejecting the idea will send it straight back.

Special interest and educational programmes
Some organisations concerned with the arts, medical research, animal health, motoring and so forth might find opportunities in the various special interest or educational programmes. Again watch the programmes and, if you see an opportunity, send off a set of notes and letter as described above.

Appearing on TV

TV is a fascinating medium. Live, intimate, technical and fast-moving are some of the adjectives used. Your first TV appearance will probably be the most nerve-racking moment of your life, next to your wedding day. Appearing on TV is an exciting experience. Enjoy it – make the most of it for yourself and your business.

TV is very much like a newspaper. It has editors and producers, who use journalists and researchers to put programmes together. The first thing you will know about being asked to appear on a programme will be a telephone call asking you to drop everything and come. Don't panic, just psyche yourself up and go through the following:

Finding out

- Ask the researcher what the story is about – are you to play a central or peripheral role?

- What is the format of the programme, documentary or discussion?
- If a discussion, is it a confrontation and if so whose side are you to be on and who else will be on the programme?
- Is the programme live or to be recorded?
- Is it to be in the studio or at your offices or in your plant?

Prepare your plan

- Plan what you want to say. The programme will involve you so make it revolve around you.
- Plan several key points that you want to make – say two good points, one that would be nice to make and one tactical point in reserve to divert the issue should the going get rough.
- Decide whether you are the most qualified person to answer for your organisation – if not *delegate*.
- Plan your schedule so that you arrive in plenty of time to have a look around the studio and meet the interviewer etc.
- Plan your appearance – what clothes you are going to wear (don't go and have a hair cut; it will make you feel self-conscious).

What to wear

- Dress naturally but soberly. Don't go out and buy a new suit (men – ensure you wear a jacket and tie – appearing offbeat loses you points with the audience).
- Be natural. Don't shave off your beard or change the colour of your hair. If you need to visit the hairdresser, just have your normal style tidied up (otherwise your friends won't recognise you). Avoid being pretentious; you will be under enough stress as it is.
- Don't wear anything which is too tight. It's going to be hot under the lights, so wear something comfortable.
- Check flies, buttons, zip. (Carry safety pin and needle and cotton.)

When you arrive

- Get there early. (Men, don't be too shy to use the cloakroom for a shave.)
- Don't drink, pop a tranquilliser or a betablocker otherwise you will come over unpredictably on the screen.

- Meet the person who invited you. Ask any questions that are troubling you.
- Get yourself shown around the studio and become familiar with the layout and routine. Listen and learn.
- Meet the interviewer and discuss the programme – like a squash warm-up, get as much information as you can without revealing your own tactics. Try to create some empathy but remember your interviewer is a *performer* and his or her job depends on the quality of work produced. If your story is worth listening to, the interviewer is going to make the most of it. The interviewer will be looking at it from the audience's point of view, that is what makes good viewing.

The interview

- If it is a recorded interview, don't start until you are absolutely ready.
- The execution chair is normally flanked by cameras and there will be one facing you.
- Look at the interviewer, not the camera.
- Fix in your mind that this is a discussion between two people – you are not a performer acting to millions.
- Bring out your points one by one, regardless of the questions being asked.
- Don't slouch or talk rapidly – the slower you take it the less you have to commit yourself.
- If you are nervous and you 'er' and 'um' or have too many 'you knows', these will be taken out of a recording.
- If it's live and you get stuck on a point, pause or polish your glasses. Don't talk for the sake of it. You can always say, 'I'm sorry. I don't know the answer to that question.'
- If you get ambushed by a long and loaded question, you can always hit back with a short and conclusive answer, leaving the interviewer with no lead into the next question.
- Don't lose your temper or play it as a verbal contest between you and the interviewer. Concentrate on your goal of putting over your image.
- Avoid a 'put down' of the interviewer as this will cause antagonism, but if you are misquoted set the record straight.
- Avoid mannerisms.

Radio interviews

Much of what has been listed in the foregoing section applies to radio, except that radio lacks the visual element and so it is necessary to use your voice more, but pauses can be used to good effect. Try talking with a laugh in your voice, particularly on telephone interviews.

Personal photograph

A good photograph of yourself is essential. From time to time the media may want to use your picture. A well-photographed picture of yourself can be used to enhance both your image and that of your organisation.

CHAPTER 9
News Release Service

Many organisations start their public relations operations by simply sending the odd story concerning their activities, to the press. With success they become more ambitious and send more stories, and quickly they discover the value of running a news release service.

The key to successful public relations is to start off with a good news release service. Get that right from the start, and it will provide a firm base on which to build a sophisticated public relations programme. For not only will good reporting of ongoing activity create interest, both with the media and the public, but as the operation develops the news release service will also become the principal means of communication with the media for special publicity activities.

One has to remember that around two-thirds of news releases sent out are not published and half of these failures are because of bad presentation; the rest fail because they are either incomplete, or in some cases dishonest.

In this chapter we will break down the news release service into three stages:

- writing a news release
- presenting and despatching
- use of photographs.

Writing a news release

Certainly any form of writing, whether it be a book, an essay or news release, presents most of us with a mental challenge. The key to writing is self-confidence and the knowledge of our own abilities. No matter how much time we spend staring at a blank sheet of paper, nothing will come until the pen starts writing. Then it takes a lot of courage to overcome the fear of rejection, especially if our first few releases have already come to nothing. So let us start out with the intention of having our first release published; there is nothing like success for motivating the writer.

First, how will the editor want to use the news release?

1. For information – it tells him about the activities of the organisation.
2. He may use the material as it is, and include it in the columns of his paper just as if one of his own staff had written it.
3. He may use it as the basis of an article or even a feature on the organisation.
4. He may simply file it and decide to use it later to support an article or feature about related subjects; for example, a release might be used in a feature on your industry's activities.

Thus, bearing these in mind, we can see straight away the need to produce a highly professional-looking piece of work which attracts the attention of editorial staff and provides sufficiently interesting information to make it worth printing.

Now, rather than staring at the blank piece of paper hoping for inspiration, let us go through a four-stage process in order to fill it with a release that will be published.

1. Obtain and write down all relevant information in note form on a sheet of paper;
2. Plan the approach and angle of the story to fit the publication and potential reader;
3. Lay out the information in a logical order putting the highlights of the story first;
4. Summarise the highlights and produce an opening paragraph which will command attention and create initial interest in the story.

Each of these stages is now explained in detail.

Get the facts

A release is not an advertisement and any writer who produces a release which is a mass of tendentious 'puffery' containing no real facts, cannot expect to see it in print. News is based on real happenings. If it is to be reported as part of a public relations operation, then it must be supported by relating the news to the activities of the organisation in such a way as to gain the attention and interest of the reader.

The writer must be able to show that he is in command of all the facts and be able to reproduce them so as to convince the reader that what is reported is both true and of interest to him. The facts needed for the average report are:

- the subject of the story (the organisation related to the activity)
- the events
- the period of time (date, time etc)
- people concerned in the story and in the pictures
- supporting evidence available or that needs to be researched
- policy of the organisation relating to the events in the story
- the benefits to the general public
- relevant statements from key people
- availability of pictures.

Aim story at publication concerned

From the outset the story must be aimed at the publication concerned. For example, a local paper expects to receive news about local people, local problems and local events, and a woman's magazine expects stories affecting or influencing its women readers.

One mistake that reduces the effectiveness of releases arises from a disregard for the requirements of types and locations of individual publications. Even at a local level, where there are say, a dozen main papers covering a county, there is a tendency for a blanket release to be sent out in an attempt to gain coverage over the whole area.

These frequently fail because each paper covers its own specific area and is mainly concerned only with the local issues affecting the immediate area of its circulation – thus news in one area is not necessarily going to be of such interest in another.

To illustrate how a story might be interpreted by different types of publications take an imaginary story of a British flying doctor who receives an award for his service in an African country.

A national newspaper might treat the subject with some emotional appeal introducing the doctor's wife at some stage and maybe his work with children.

A local paper from the doctor's home town, would emphasise that he came from the town and would include his school, his relatives still living in the town and any organisations that he may have belonged to.

Specialist magazine (eg the *Geographical Magazine*) would treat the subject by examining geographical, cultural and anthropological aspects of the story.

Angle the story
In determining the approach with regard to the specific requirements of certain publications, we may well have gone some way to angling the story. However, the basic theme of the story need not only be expressed by presenting the cold facts. Bearing in mind the publication and its readers, try and present a novel angle that will appeal to them; especially those we particularly want to interest. An example could be a report about a sponsored event run by a local company where a cold factual report might make a couple of column inches; yet a story about the boy who won the first prize, with suitable pictures, might gain a half-page or even more.

A recent, real example of a news release writer angling a story to create maximum interest occurred when a company organised a visit for a boys' club to a first division football club. The members had the chance to train with the players as well as collecting autographs. This in itself would have produced a reasonable story capable of gaining the attention of younger male readers. However, during the training one of the boys managed to score a goal past the team's famous goalkeeper. The release was angled around the boy's achievement and, with a photograph, gained the front page of the local paper with consequent publicity for the company.

Lay out the facts
Having gathered the information and planned the angle of the story, make a rough layout. Put the story into a logical sequence of events; this is not necessarily a chronological sequence, but one which will gain and hold the interest of the reader.

Summarise the highlights
The highlights should come at the beginning, the reasons and explanations then being fitted in to build a logical story. Make the first paragraph demand attention. Many writers, particularly new ones, are guilty of writing into the subject. By starting off with an idea they hope that sooner or later they will start the story, for example.

> Every year, at about this time, Sunley has its annual carnival. The event draws scores of entries from local organisations, industry and even private individuals. One such entry was the float provided by Bolt and Shaddon Limited.

Figure 9.1 *The illustration shows how effectively a simple photograph and press story can be used to make a news item in the trade press. Also, the regional display unit from Ideal Standard demonstrates how a little creative thinking can produce a useful marketing tool.* (Permission of Heating Ventilating Plumbing and Ideal Standard)

Compare the above with an opening paragraph that demands attention and interest, by starting with the highlight of the story and by introducing the subject and the organisation very early in the first sentence.

> This year's winning entry for the best float at the Sunley Carnival was one featuring scouting history; it was designed and built by the Sunley Scout Group and sponsored by Bolt and Shaddon Limited, well known in the county for horticultural supplies.

The first paragraph should summarise the key elements of the story and provide sufficient information to motivate the reader to read the complete item.

Length of the release
Releases should rarely exceed 500 words, but the new writer might be content with 250 until he has gained experience.

Headlines
There is no need to produce a headline. The editor will do this to fit in with his page make-up. Simply write a short title, to show what the story is about.

Use a journalistic style
The acceptable style, appropriate to all publications, is good clear English which is neither 'stiff nor racy' that flows easily and uses words economically. This is journalistic style, which allows speed and ease of reading so that news and ideas can quickly be assimilated by the reader. Always write in the past tense and in the third person except, of course, for speech and quotations.

Examples of this style are found in the news columns of newspapers and magazines and it can only be emphasised that constant reading of these will be of real assistance to the new writer. Copy out a few columns from a good paper and try to get the style – with practice it will give a professional edge to release writing.

Punctuation
Poor punctuation is frequently the downfall of many releases. There is a surprising level of bad punctuation with such elementary mistakes as 'its' and 'it's', and over-use of commas making sentences long and complex. Keep sentences fairly short; this helps to loosen up the style and makes for easier reading. The writer who lacks confidence in his ability to use punctuation, needs to borrow a book

on English grammar, or writing, from the library, and revise.

Adjectives
Use them sparingly and be particularly careful about using such adjectives as 'monstrous', 'massive', 'mammoth', and so forth, which exaggerate. The word 'unique', should not be used unless the subject is indeed unique, and equally, use alternatives for such expressions as 'almost unique'.

Use adjectives only where a noun needs qualifying for the purpose of communication – such as 'challenging experience' – but not to advertise the organisation's 'luxurious premises'. If the sense of luxury, toughness etc is to be put over, do it in the story by phrases in the copy so that the reader cannot help but gain the right impression.

Tendentiousness
Never attempt to advertise. Editors receive daily news releases which end: 'The organisation needs more members, anyone interested should contact . . .' or '. . . Liberals – the party to vote for'. Use the news release to create interest and maintain a mutual understanding with the general public; that is what it is for.

Bathos and pomposity
Neither has a place in news release writing. One of the unfortunate aspects of non-professional writers is that, like people who give talks, their minds occasionally run away with them and they become self-indulgent to the detriment of the work they produce.

Cynicism
Cynicism is a self-indulgent habit which should not occur in news releases. To editors and readers alike, it conjures up a picture of an immature mind at work. If there are aspects of life, affecting the organisation that are viewed with cynicism, by all means produce arguments against them, but allow the reader to form his own views on the basis of the evidence produced.

Statistics/Tables
Always summarise statistics. Do not expect editors to use long complicated tables, for example, this hypothetical example of a survey of traffic down a narrow road was produced by a ratepayers' association:

	Cars	Lorries	Other vehicles	Total
8.00–9.00	100	30	20	150
9.00–10.00	100	60	5	165
10.00–11.00	20	60	5	85

Instead of producing the table try:

> The busiest time in the road is between 8.00 and 10.00 with traffic increasing from 150 to 165 vehicles an hour. One of the most objectionable features is the hourly rise in heavy lorries, ranging from 30 an hour at 9.00 to 60 by 11.00 am.

Presentation and despatching

Having looked at writing releases, we should now pay as much attention to presentation. A badly produced release not only gives the editor a poor impression of the writer, but also wastes his time, especially if he has to pore over an unreadable word or make numerous corrections to shoddy work.

Paper

Use white, A4 size, top-copy quality or a reasonable duplicating paper, never flimsy paper.

Most businesses produce their own printed-heading news release paper; this draws attention to the release and the editor immediately identifies it for what it is. The design of the heading should be simple yet bold, but be careful of cluttering the top of the sheet with an over-ornate design or too much copy; simply use the words: 'NEWS', 'NEWS RELEASE' or 'NEWS BULLETIN'. The question of whether to put the name of the organisation in a prominent situation at the top of the sheet, or less prominent at the bottom, really depends on the length of the name. Some organisations manage to incorporate their names or initials successfully in the title of the release. The overriding factor is whether the editor receiving the release will know immediately what it is and where it originated.

It is, however, necessary to have the full name and address somewhere on the release, including day and night telephone numbers, in order that the press can contact the author at any time.

Typing

Having written good releases, a number of organisations place them at a disadvantage through bad typing. Even a professional secretary will need some direction. Work for the press is typed differently from the usual business letter or document, and it is important to follow certain rules:

1. Use double-line spacing.
2. Precede all paragraphs with an extra space and indent them. (This makes it easier to read and allows space for editorial remarks etc.)
3. Leave at least 1½ inches between the heading and first words of the release (to allow for the editor's remarks and headline).
4. No underlinings should appear anywhere in the release (in printing, this means 'print in italics' and it is the editorial department's prerogative to decide on emphasis).
5. Sheets should be typed on one side only.
6. If it is necessary to follow on to another sheet the word 'more' should appear at the bottom of the preceding sheet. All sheets should be numbered. The copy should conclude with the word 'end'. This practice ensures that the reader sees the whole story and helps to prevent sheets going astray in a busy news office.
7. Use only black ribbon; there is no need to type titles or key points in red.

Duplicating

Photocopies are usually accepted.

Folding and posting

Use standard, foolscap wallet envelopes and allow the release to be folded in one direction only. This ensures that there are only two folds in the sheet. Never force the release into an envelope too small for it.

Despatch on time

A number of news release services fall down because there is a laxity about sending out material. One organisation was on the point of discontinuing its release service because material was not being used, when it was discovered that the publicity manager was 'sitting' on the news, and totally disregarding the fact that by the time it arrived on the editor's desk, it was worthlessly out of date; and, of course, there are the stories of the willing typist who enthusiastically rushes away to type a news release, and then returns the work weeks later when, alas, it is too late for publication.

Weekly papers
If publishing on Friday, the weekly paper must have the material in by the time it goes to press: this means usually by Wednesday afternoon and only exceptionally Thursday morning for urgent, important news. (If the paper publishes earlier in the week, work out the 'going to press' time by subtracting a day and a half.) It is worth checking with the editorial department to ensure the latest dates for publication. Keep a card for each publication with name of editor, lead time etc (see Chapter 11).

Daily papers, television and radio
These media receive news the day after the event has happened. If there is any doubt that this will be achieved for urgent news, telephone the release through.

Magazines
Most magazines have long lead times (that is, material may need to be received six to eight weeks prior to publication date). Therefore material must often be sent out before the news actually happens, with an embargo on it (if it is guaranteed), or afterwards, in a style that will not make it sound out of date.

Embargoes
Occasionally, as with the appointment of a new chairman, presentation of accounts or a release to a magazine with a long lead time, it may not be desirable for news to reach the public before a certain date. Therefore write at the top of the release:

'NOT FOR PUBLICATION BEFORE . . .'

Embargoes should only be used when conditions present no alternative.

Use of titles and letters
Using letters after people's names is unnecessary. Editors usually ignore BA, BSc, and so forth, unless they have a direct bearing on the story. However, they will always want the correct title: Doctor, PC, Sir, Lord etc. Check with the person's office or secretary that the title in the release is correct, to save any embarrassment for both the press and the organisation.

The Wincanton Historic Commercial Vehicle Run

London to Brighton First Sunday in May

Please reply to:
Mike Daly
Publicity Profile Ltd
Tel: 01 240 1042

Press Release No. 18/283a/83

28th February 19XX

LONDON TO BRIGHTON ON MAY 5th

The annual Wincanton Historic Commercial Vehicle Run from London to Brighton will take place on Sunday May 5th 1985.

There are a record number of entrants in this year's Run, which is being sponsored by the Wincanton Transport group for the fourth consecutive year, with a marvellous variety of the world's finest examples of historic commercials. These range from three wheel road sweepers to fire engines, by way of steamers, lorries of all shapes and sizes, buses, military vehicles and taxis.

The oldest vehicle in this year's Run is an 1886 Marshall traction engine, owned by Peter Fagg of Shoreham by Sea in Sussex. The owner reckons it will take twelve hours to make the trip, so rather than start on Sunday morning, he will be setting off at midnight, in order to be at Brighton around midday on Sunday!

From further afield there is a 1939 Citroen pick up from Holland, a 1931 Chevrolet lorry from Jersey, a 1935 Bedford tanker from Eire and a 1947 Bedford van from Edinburgh which is still in daily use as a delivery vehicle. Lord Montagu, president of the HCVS, will be driving his 1922 Maxwell Charabanc and his son, the Hon Ralph Montagu, will be driving a 1947 Land Rover for the first time in the event.

Cont.../

Figure 9.2

> Press Release No. 18/283a/83 Cont.../
>
> The 200 plus entrants will leave Battersea Park, London between 6.30 - 9.30 in the morning of the 5th, taking the A23 via Crawley (where they make a stop by the railway station) down to Brighton. Vehicles will arrive there from around 10.30am and will line up along Madeira Drive for judging; with prize giving taking place at 4.00pm.
>
> The Wincanton Group, which celebrates its Diamond Jubilee this year, will again be playing host to about 100 children from the Variety Club, and a well known TV personality will be there on the day to make the whole event a special day out.
>
> Battersea Park, the A23 or Brighton on May 5th are the places to be for anyone with even a passing interest in old commercial vehicles.
>
> -- Ends --

Use of photographs

It is often said that a good photograph is worth a thousand words of copy. Yet photography is expensive and, alas, all too frequently photographs sent out are not used.

Like stories, photographs need to appeal to the reader. They should command attention and generate interest in the subject. This can be achieved by showing action; for example, someone who won a prize for a high jump could be going over the bar rather than standing holding his medal. Another way is by introducing elements of human interest that appeal to the emotion of the reader by, say, introducing animals, children, pretty girls or old soldiers into the pictures. A sponsored event might be illustrated by the picture of a young child taking part, rather than with a panoramic photograph of the event. Where possible, introduce people into pictures; not in rows of unsmiling mannequins, but have them enthusiastically taking part in the activity being reported.

All photographs sent out should have a caption explaining the event and naming the key people in the picture. As well as sending out photographs with news releases they can be mailed out on their own (plus the caption) as a 'photo-caption' release. The caption should summarise the story in much the same way as the opening paragraph of a news release; but as it tells the news story it should completely satisfy the reader's interest by furnishing him with sufficient

PRESS INFORMATION

For further press information please contact:

Traverway Holdings Limited
398 Seven Sisters Road
London N42LX
Tel: (01) 802 0927
Telex: 291805

Publicity Profile Limited
141/143 Drury Lane
London WC2
Tel: 01-240 1042

RELEASE NO. 61/015/09   18 August 1986

TRAVERWAY LAUNCH NEW SERVICE

Traverway Maritime, who have operated a conventional service from Northern Europe to the Eastern Mediterranean for nearly a decade, have expanded this operation and are now also offering a direct service from Spain to the East Med.

Initially the sailings will be monthly from Bilbao and Valencia to Beirut, Lattakia and Mersin, from where on-carriage is available to Iran and Iraq.

TML have appointed as Agents in Spain for this new service Martico s.l. Berastegui4, P.O. Box 940, Bilbao. Tel: 4475600. Tlx: 31025 MATLE. UK enquiries for this new service and for the existing service from the Northern European ports of Shoreham, Antwerp and Rotterdam should be addressed to Martin Turner at Traverway House in London. Tel: 01-802 0927.

--- ENDS ---

Press Contact: Mike Daly at PPL on 01-240 1042

Figure 9.3

information. Captions should usually be kept to around 50 words and only occasionally as many as 80.

Do not write on the photographs. Some photographs are spoiled by being written on. Ball-point or even fountain pen will show through from the back, thus preventing reproduction. There are two ways of captioning:

1. Type the caption on a gummed label and stick it to the back of the photograph.
2. Sellotape a sheet of paper, with the caption typed on it, to the back of the photograph in order that the caption appears under the face of the photograph.

There are merits in both methods, but the first is usually preferred, unless the caption is a long one.

Sending out pictures

Size: Half plate (6½ × 4½in) is the best and most economical size to send out. Any smaller and they will not reproduce well; larger ones are likely to be damaged in the post.

Quality: Always use sharp, contrasting pictures to ensure that the detail comes through on newsprint.

Finish: Prints for reproduction should be glossy.

Colour pictures: Photographs should always be black and white. Colour prints, however attractive they may look, are not normally accepted, as the problems in reproduction outweigh their usefulness.

If a publication does have colour facilities it might be possible to persuade the editor to use a colour transparency (larger than 35mm) but this should be negotiated.

Posting: Never fold or roll pictures. Send them flat in an adequately sized envelope protected with cardboard. Do not use paper clips, staples, or anything else which may mark or damage the photograph.

Reporters

Many non-professional publicity people tend to worry about reporters, and occasionally working relationships fail because either they are not completely honest with the reporters or they unwittingly create the wrong impression by putting up a false front.

Reporters and journalists, by and large, are constantly working against time 'to get the paper out'. Thus the publicity manager who makes any reporter's life easier will certainly earn his gratitude.

If reporters attend events then the publicity manager must always be readily available – not running the raffle – and should have adequately prepared notes to assist them. If interviews are required, then he should either have proposed interviewees easily on hand, or be interviewed himself. He should be prepared, and have the authority to commit himself as a spokesman for the organisation, and should never have to ring up the reporter the next day to change his story.

Whatever the event, if the press are expected, be available to talk to them. If necessary have a central press office (tent, caravan etc) to which reporters can be directed.

Photographers

There are two categories of photographer, other than the good amateur, that the publicity manager is likely to work with.

The press photographer

He may be working alongside a reporter, in which case the reporter will direct him, or as agency photographer, he may come along on his own. In the latter capacity, he may well be doing a minor reporting job as well; that is, making notes which will form the basis of the captions.

A photographer working on his own can be greatly assisted by the publicity manager. Most press photographers have to work against a deadline. They like to take their photographs as quickly as possible and get back to their office to process them. Thus the publicity manager can assist the photographer with ideas, and by quickly organising people into participating, the photographs can be taken quickly and the photographer can get away.

All photographers have a sense of mischief, and no disrespect is implied, as at some time or other we have all had a laugh at a humorous photograph; the Mayoress's skirt blossoming in the wind, or the microphone collapsing. If, however, the organisation is one which tries to create the image of smartness and efficiency, it is as well to make it quite clear to everyone that untidy uniform, 'hands in pockets' athletes, or children smoking, are quickly spotted by a critical reader.

Hired photographer

A lot of money is wasted on photography, chiefly by the late delivery of photographs. Some companies have been known to take months to supply pictures and this is simply not on; photographs, like news releases, must be despatched on time. Make it quite clear, when booking a photographer, that prints are required within 24 hours for the press. If they do not arrive – *do not pay*.

Many publicity people make the mistake of letting the photographer 'get on with it'; consequently, there are few usable pictures. Go as far as writing out a 'shooting schedule' even with hand-drawn sketches to show the photographer. Make sure that the photographer fully understands that the pictures must be suitable for publication.

Most photographers retain negatives and claim the copyright on their pictures. Make it quite clear to the photographer that the organisation is 'employing' him to take pictures for general release to the press and press agencies, and that you take full responsibility for distribution. This ensures that he can neither charge royalties nor sell copies of photographs to the public or press without prior permission. There is no point in paying an attendance fee and allowing the photographer to make a further profit from selling the photographs. He will, of course, charge for the prints.

CHAPTER 10
Financial Planning of Promotional Activity

Too many organisations do not spend enough on promoting themselves. Others spend wastefully. Yet many successful entrepreneurs have found that by good planning, money invested in the promotion of the business really contributes to growth and profitability. The successful entrepreneur is one who thinks of promotional expenditure as an investment rather than as a mere cost.

It is the aim of efective promotion to create a dialogue between the organisation and those people it seeks to influence, namely customers, backers, employees and the community as a whole. The better the dialogue the more influential the organisation becomes. It follows that the better the planning that goes into promoting your business the more effective it is likely to be. Planning the financial side is therefore very important if sufficient funds are to be allocated to the promotional tasks which you will be designing to achieve your objectives.

Look at the big picture

Stand back, look at the big picture of your business. Think about the direction in which you want it to go. As a successful achiever you are probably already thinking financially in terms of one year, two years, even five years ahead. In the process of building your own business you will spend quite a lot promoting it. The question 'How much?' should be replaced by 'What is to be achieved?'

Seeing the big picture of the business will enable you to identify and set priorities for what you need to do to grow your business successfully. For example, you may need to launch new products or services, capture new customers, raise money or recruit good quality people. Your promotional activity is what is going to help you to

Financial Planning of Promotional Activity

create the sort of awareness and receptivity that will win support for your cause.

Methods of allocating money to promotion

Money reserved for promotion is called the 'promotional appropriation'. The question of how to decide on the right amount of reserve has traditionally been answered through presenting the following alternatives:

- Decide on a percentage of sales and calculate your appropriation accordingly. Distributors of other people's products are often given a percentage discount with which to promote their principal's products. The advantage is simplicity and ease of accounting. The difficulties are in finding the right percentage with the dangers of under- or over-spending. Furthermore, if sales go down so does the appropriation, which is perhaps just the time when more should be spent.
- Plus up last year's expenses by a percentage to include inflation and possibly business growth. This method is probably quite appropriate for a fairly mature business which is not subject to the dynamics of intense competition. This method is, however, too inflexible for the growth organisation. The reason is that it ignores tasks and objectives. In effect, you would have to fit your tasks and objectives into the available appropriation. It should seem more sensible to create an appropriation to meet predetermined tasks and objectives.
- The third traditional method is to cost out the various tasks and campaigns that the organisation wishes to undertake and set an appropriation to meet them. The advantage of this method is that it is related directly to the objectives set. The disadvantages are that there may be, on a year-to-year basis, tremendous increases or decreases in promotional costs. Furthermore, there is a danger that too many short-term projects may be initiated to the detriment of overall profitability.

In trying to find a method that would be suitable for the small business, the effective route would have the following characteristics:

- It is related to tasks and objectives.
- It is flexible.
- It is based on a longer-term business development strategy.

- It allows the business to grow within its capabilities and availability of resources.

The method therefore recommended is as follows:

- Look at the big picture and identify the projects that need to be accomplished over a time frame of say one, two and five years.
- Cost the projects and build up a longer-term cost and revenue picture for each.
- Set priorities over, say, a five-year period and feed the projects in as resources, time and finances permit.
- Plan your promotional costs around the projects that you have selected and project them through the same five-year period.

By looking at the big picture you will begin to see the sort of levels of expenditure that you are likely to need for the future. The need for promotional expenditure and the levels at which it should be spent will become apparent once you can determine where you want to take your business in the future.

Payback calculations

Some projects take longer to return a profit than others; consequently, you will need to make some forecast on the returns from the funds invested. For one-off projects such as an exhibition stand it may be easier to calculate the payback than for a major new product launch which may take years, as the examples below show:

Exhibition	£
Stand rental	2,000
Design and display costs	2,000
Samples	1,000
Literature	1,500
Other costs	500
	7,000

To break even sufficient business would need to be generated to cover the £7000 invested.

Financial Planning of Promotional Activity

For a major launch of a new product or service considerable sums will need to be invested to gain sufficient awareness and trial among targeted consumers. Here it may take several years before a payback is achieved, for example.

Years	1	2	3	4	5
Sales	10,000	15,000	20,000	25,000	30,000
Less cost of goods	5,000	7,500	10,000	12,500	15,000
Gross profit	5,000	7,500	10,000	12,500	15,000
Less promotional costs	8,000	8,000	8,000	8,000	8,000
Profit/(loss)	(3,000)	(500)	2,000	4,500	7,000
Cumulative profit/(loss)	(3,000)	(3,500)	(1,500)	3,000	10,000

As you can see in the example, it is not until the fourth year that the example goes into profit – that is, it pays back.

Setting budgets

Revenue and expense budgets should ideally be set for each financial year. An effective way is to divide the year into monthly financial periods for which sales, expenses and fund flows are targeted. By comparing actual results at the end of each financial period with your target (budget) you can gain an accurate impression of how well your business is performing and expenses are being controlled. Another value of budgeting is that it sets targets throughout the organisation. Everyone is then working to a common set of objectives.

The example on page 128 illustrates how the budget can be compared with actual revenue and expenses. The example takes a business three months into a financial year.

Budgeting your promotional expenditure is essential if you are to keep a tight control on outgoings. A useful way is to budget each item of expenditure and at best you can stick to what you have planned. One thing you will find is that if you lose track of expenses then promotional costs can easily run away with your money. It's best therefore to get a grip of expenses at the outset by good forward planning.

If you are running monthly budgets then use each month to review your expenses. You want to be able to answer these questions:

1. How much have I spent so far?
2. How much is committed?
3. How much is left of the budget to spend?

ABC Company March/three months/cumulative

	Actual £	Budget £	Variance £
Sales	20,000	21,000	(1,000)
Cost of goods	10,000	10,500	500
Gross profit	10,000	10,500	(500)
Less promotional expenses	3,000	3,000	—
Contribution after promotion	7,000	7,500	(500)
Less: Selling costs	2,000	2,000	—
Distribution costs	1,000	1,200	200
Administration costs	2,000	2,000	—
Operating Profit	2,000	2,300	300

The following example shows a way of keeping summary records to facilitate control and monitoring of promotional expenses:

Item	Actual to date £	Budget for year £	Committed to year end £	Balance to year end £
Advertising	10,000	30,000	20,000	Nil
PR	3,000	5,000	—	2,000
Promotion	4,000	8,000	2,000	2,000
Research	1,000	1,000	—	—
Exhibitions	6,000	12,000	6,000	—
Artwork	4,000	2,000	—	(2,000)
Other	4,000	8,000	1,000	3,000
Total	32,000	66,000	29,000	5,000

Life would be too easy if you could run a business exactly to a budget formula but, of course, you cannot. Periodically you would need to review your activity and update plans in the light of results or changes in market conditions. Very often you will have to totally change a set

Financial Planning of Promotional Activity 129

of plans and incorporate changes to expenses. Here the value of accurate expense reviews becomes apparent. If you have to make a radical change in direction, knowing what has been spent, committed and what is left can be very important.

Cut-off points

It's easy to assume that every promotional project is going to work. You will get failures. The trick in avoiding a major disaster is to plan ahead so that you meet *decision points* beyond which you can decide whether to continue with your plan, change direction or cut your losses. Build decision points into your planning and ensure you commit your funds only as far as each one. Review each project thoroughly at the appropriate decision point. Be objective; do not simply cut off because you have lost interest or because you suddenly need cash for another part of the business. Successful promotion requires continuity, sometimes for years.

CHAPTER 11
Media Planning

The word *media* describes the means through which target audiences and interest groups can be reached.

There are six mainstream media through which advertisers and public relations managers can reach their audiences:

- television
- press
- radio
- cinema
- posters
- direct mail.

Mainstream media

The principal feature of all the mainstream media and the data we have about them is their importance to national advertisers. With something in excess of 2 billion pounds a year spent on advertising in the UK, the industry attempts to gear itself to appeal to the national advertiser. Yet in structure much of the mainstream media is regional in nature: commercial TV, commercial radio, cinema, posters and much of the press are in fact local. This feature of mainstream media allows them to be used by small firms with quite modest budgets. The availability of special interest magazines also enables local firms to reach national audiences which are very specific - such as boating or yachting enthusiasts. Direct mail is a highly targetable medium and can be directed at large local or specialist audiences.

Television
The attraction of TV is its very high penetration of homes and

potential audiences. In a single week 90 per cent of all individuals will watch TV. The main feature of TV advertising is its ability to build up cover and frequency very quickly with a message which is both auditory and visual.

Television is a distinctly down-market medium. It is watched more by the old than the young and is very female-oriented. For those products which are universally purchased this may not be a major problem but if you are trying to sell offfice computers, expensive cars or medical insurance the issue of targeting and buying a specific type of air times becomes extremely important. Fortunately the TV companies have an excellent knowledge of their audiences and are able to guide you on the best times to buy spots for your specific audiences.

There are 13 TV areas in the UK reaching some 20 million homes – 98 per cent of all homes have a TV. The breakdown is shown in the table below.

Television – areas and costs

Area	Net ITV homes in area	
	000	%
London	4,045	19.73
Midlands	3,129	15.26
North West	2,450	11.95
Yorkshire	2,110	10.29
C Scotland	1,256	6.13
Wales & West	1,580	7.71
South & S. East/Channel	1,839	8.97
North East	1,064	5.19
East of England	1,315	6.41
S West	586	2.86
Ulster	464	2.26
Border	242	1.18
N E Scotland	423	2.06
Network	20,503	100.00

Costs		Household penetration of	
Estimated annual average network costs per 100 TVRS (30")		Any TV set	98%
		Colour TV sets	90%
		2 or more TV sets	50%
Housewives:	£132,000	VCR	44%
Adults:	£156,000	Teletext	18%
Men:	£180,000	Remote Control TV	39%
Women:	£142,000	Subscription/Cable	1%

Sources: Based on BARB Establishment Surveys NRS and RMP estimates
By permission of Ray Morgan and Partners

The introduction of Channel 4 has given national advertisers an opportunity to target far more selectively, although it must be remembered that downmarket older viewers still form the larger part of the audience, even if Channel 4 is relatively more upmarket than ITV. Note also that total hours viewed run in favour of ITV with 85 per cent as against Channel 4.

Teletext
Teletext televisions are present in over 4 million homes in Great Britain, with circulation increasing at an average rate of 70,000 new sets each month. Teletext therefore outsells all national daily newspapers.

The BBC call their Teletext service CEEFAX, a play on the words 'See facts'. ITV's service ORACLE stands for Optional Reception of Announcements by Coded Line Electronics. Teletext differs from any other medium in that the consumer has total control in deciding which information to look at and when to look at it. The service is also the most up to date available.

CEEFAX
Both BBC1 and BBC2 have this service. BBC1 carries the instant news magazine along with finance, weather and travel, BBC information, TV and radio and a series of further pages including recipes, farm prices and transmitter information. BBC2 also carries news but concentrates in greater detail on the more important issues of the day.

The service is on the air 365 days of the year throughout all the programme hours listed in the *Radio Times*. Up-to-date information is gathered in the newsroom at TV Centre from such sources as Reuters and various press associations.

CEEFAX, being part of the BBC, carries no advertising. CEEFAX also transmits telesoftware programs specifically for the BBC Micro; a special downloading unit is necessary to use such a service.

The future holds the possibility of transmitting quality pictures similar to those found in colour magazines. A memory bank is also being developed retaining pages for immediate recall.

ORACLE
ORACLE is a free-to-use service, differing from the Prestel Viewdata service which needs a telephone line to link into the information source.

This up-to-date service ranges from news coverage to competitions and from financial information to the consumers' daily horoscopes.

ORACLE carries over 350 indexed source pages, containing both national and regional information and advertising. The national service is on the air from 6.30am until close of television transmission. Regional information is available from 9.30am, ie the end of TV AM until the end of transmission. Both ITV and Channel 4 carry ORACLE. News information coming from a team of journalists at ITN, together with the TV guide and sport pages, are the most widely used of the services available to ITV ORACLE viewers. The City and Financial page is the most popular service offered on Channel 4, reflected in the fact that a 3.4 million ORACLE adult audience have viewed the Foreign Exchange pages and 3 million the Share Price page.

Further pages offered on ITV include a travel information service with a direct line with the AA, British Rail, British Airways and London Transport. ORACLE also carries pages with information on the weather, racing and spare time activities.

ORACLE entertains an average daily audience of over 3 million adults and is growing. Adverts placed on either the national or regional networks can reap the benefits of such a consistently large viewing audience; 8 million adults claim to have seen advertising on ORACLE.

Advertising on TV is extremely expensive but it can really add sales to your business. TV advertising also adds to the credibility and standing of a business. A whole basket of opportunities is available for the local advertiser including discounts, help with production and special deals. The advertising manager of your regional station is well worth talking to.

Press

National newspapers
There are about 10 national daily newspapers and eight Sunday papers, together with the *Scotsman* and the *Irish Times* which reach some 70 per cent of the UK audience. All newspapers have distinct class and age profiles. In terms of class they range from the *Financial Times* whose readership is 87 per cent ABC1 to the Star with 18 per cent. Age profiles are not quite so pronounced but are still very significant. Newspapers such as the *Guardian* and *Daily Telegraph* with similar class profiles can be totally different in terms of age bias with 47 per cent of the *Guardian's* readers aged 15–34 while only 23 per cent of the *Telegraph's* fall in this age range.

Press – costs, coverage and readership profile tables
READERSHIP PROFILE – ALL ADULTS

National Newspapers	Page Cost mono (ROP/ROW) £	Circulation 000	Adult Coverage %	Men %	Women %	H/W (Female) %	15–34 %	35–54 %	55+ %	ABC1 %	C2DE %
The Sun	23,562	4,050	26	53	47	39	46	30	24	25	75
Daily Mirror	21,300	3,139	20	55	45	37	39	29	32	25	75
Daily Mail	18,900	1,732	11	52	48	41	35	31	34	56	44
Daily Express	18,865	1,729	10	53	47	40	30	33	37	50	50
The Star	8,575	1,278	10	59	41	32	52	27	21	18	82
Daily Telegraph	24,640	1,132	6	54	46	39	27	35	38	83	17
The Guardian	14,000	507	3	62	38	32	47	35	18	80	20
The Times	11,500	467	3	58	42	35	38	40	22	85	15
Today	3,600	307	2	59	41	33	51	31	18	48	52
Financial Times	18,368	190	2	71	29	22	41	41	18	86	14
The Independent	7,500	—	—	—	—	—	—	—	—	—	—
News of the World	24,990	4,954	29	50	50	41	44	29	27	25	75
Sunday Mirror	22,770	3,046	21	51	49	40	42	31	27	28	72
The People	20,550	2,983	19	52	48	40	38	31	31	27	73
Sunday Express	36,000	2,181	14	52	48	41	30	30	40	58	42
Mail on Sunday	17,900	1,601	11	51	49	38	46	32	22	58	42
Sunday Times	29,00	1,147	8	55	45	38	42	38	20	79	21
Observer	18,500	769	5	55	45	38	43	35	22	76	24
Sunday Telegraph	17,920	686	5	53	47	41	30	33	37	78	22
Sunday Today	3,900	231	2	58	42	32	55	30	15	53	47

Sources: NRS Jan–Dec 1986   ABC Jul–Dec 1986

By permission of Ray Morgan and Partners

Magazines

The UK boasts a great diversity of magazines, with national distribution which enhances the possibilities of specific targeting. For example, about 35 magazines are devoted to motoring.

Magazine buying is very female oriented and there are at least eight publications with circulations in excess of over half a million. Several have very similar age and class profiles but there are opportunities for fairly specific audience targeting.

For the younger woman there are titles such as *Cosmopolitan*, *Company* and *Options*, while for the upmarket woman there are magazines such as *Vogue* and *Harpers and Queen*.

Men tend not to be so keen on buying and reading magazines as women. There are, however, a wide range of titles available for targeting a particular type of male audience. For example, if you were trying to reach AB businessmen with a colour advertisement then the *Observer*, *Sunday Telegraph* and *Sunday Times* colour supplements might form part of a schedule. *The Economist*, *Golf World*, *Yachting*, and *Punch* would also reach the same audience.

Regional daily papers

Such a paper is the *Yorkshire Post*, which has been in existence since 1754. Although essentially a north-eastern paper, it is widely read by Yorkshire people everywhere. The *Birmingham Post* is another well-established provincial daily; however, its circulation tends to be confined to the Midlands. Others papers in this group include the *Western Daily Press*, the *Northern Echo*, and the Eastern Daily Press.

All these papers have a strong regional influence and so, as well as reporting national news, they tend also to reflect the news and views of their regions. They are therefore of great value to many organisations within their circulation areas.

Local evening papers

In London there is the *Evening Standard* which absorbed the *Standard*, established in 1827.

There are now well over 50 regional newspapers in the country, many of them less than 30 years old, such as the *Watford Echo*, which covers south Hertfordshire and parts of Buckinghamshire and Berkshire. There are, however, still a number of the older papers such as the *Derby Evening Telegraph* which goes back to 1879 and *Wolverhampton Express and Star* which was established in 1874.

This group of papers mainly devotes its front pages to national

Women's Magazines	Page cost FM Mono £	Colour £	Circulation 000	Female coverage Women %	H/W % (Female)	Readership profile – women 15–34 %	35–54 %	55+ %	ABC1 %	C2DE %
WOMEN'S WEEKLY PERIODICALS (over 500,000 Circulation)										
Womans Own	13,000	18,300	1,044	19	18	45	30	25	41	59
Woman	11,400	16,100	996	14	14	48	29	23	43	57
Womans Weekly	7,100	10,100	1,164	13	13	27	31	42	41	59
Womans Realm	5,300	7,400	605	8	9	29	33	38	40	60
My Weekly	2,760	4,150	616	8	8	22	33	45	33	67
The People's Friend	1,820	2,710	578	7	7	15	26	59	28	72
Chat	3,850	6,500	591	5	4	55	27	18	25	75
WOMEN'S MONTHLY BI-MONTHLY AND QUARTERLY PERIODICALS (over 150,000 Circulation)										
Family Circle	5,925	9,220	576	11	11	38	40	22	49	51
Woman and Home	4,770	7,950	544	9	10	25	34	41	54	46
Good Housekeeping	4,800	7,487	332	9	10	34	35	31	63	37
Hair (Quarterly)	1,260	2,850	210	8	6	73	20	7	43	57
Cosmopolitan	4,539	6,837	348	7	5	67	25	8	62	38
Ideal Home	3,300	5,460	195	7	5	40	35	25	56	44
Living	3,295	5,280	354	5	7	42	41	17	56	44
Homes and Gardens	2,890	4,840	183	5	6	23	38	39	67	33
Slimming (Bi-Monthly)	2,000	3,500	248	4	4	52	36	12	45	55
Womans Journal	2,400	3,575	208	4	4	35	32	33	67	33
Home and Freezer Digest	1,960	3,050	201	4	5	29	44	27	50	50
She	2,464	4,730	195	4	4	47	36	17	59	41
Options	2,552	3,470	215	3	3	64	26	10	64	36
Elle	2,750	3,850	204	3	2	69	22	9	71	29
Womans World	1,950	3,300	202	3	3	57	22	21	45	55
Company	2,710	4,500	170	2	1	80	15	5	66	34

Source: NRS Jan-Dec 1986 ABC Jul-Dec 1986

By permission of Ray Morgan and Partners.

General periodicals (over 100,000 circulation)	Page cost F/M Mono £	Colour £	Circulation 000	Adult Coverage %	Readership Profile—all adults							
					Men %	Women %	H/W % (Female)	15–34 %	35–54 %	55+ %	ABC1 %	C2DE %
Sunday (W)	27,500	31,000	4,594	26	49	51	42	44	29	27	25	75
Radio Times (W)	13,200	22,000	3,233	21	46	54	45	40	30	30	49	51
TV Times (W)	12,750	21,200	3,186	21	46	54	45	43	30	27	43	57
Readers Digest (M)	8,600	11,820	1,506	15	51	49	43	31	37	32	50	50
Sunday Express Magazine (W)	19,250	24,300	2,181	13	51	49	42	30	30	40	58	42
You (Mail on Sunday) (W)	10,650	14,675	1,601	11	50	50	39	46	32	22	58	42
Sunday Times Magazine (W)	11,000	17,000	1,147	8	54	46	38	43	38	19	78	22
Observer Magazine (W)	6,600	9,900	769	6	54	46	38	43	35	22	76	24
Sunday Telegraph Magazine (W)	5,566	6,655	686	5	52	48	42	30	33	37	78	22
Smash Hits (F)	4,650	7,950	481	5	46	54	20	84	15	1	38	62
Exchange and Mart (W)	1,682	–	216	5	76	24	20	54	33	13	41	59
Weekly News (W)	3,552	–	785	4	40	60	53	25	31	44	25	75
What Car (M)	1,640	3,795	125*	4	82	18	14	63	27	10	55	45
Private Eye (F)	2,400	–	226*	3	69	31	24	60	31	9	76	24
Fiesta (M)	2,300	2,300	251*	2	93	7	7	59	36	5	28	72
Mayfair (M)	1,760	2,640	171*	2	92	8	7	58	36	6	37	63
Weekend (W)	3,700	5,500	271*	2	35	65	53	41	34	25	34	66
Titbits (M)	1,680	2,450	138*	2	43	57	46	42	37	21	28	72
Motorcycle News (W)	2,507	2,650	133	2	84	16	13	68	24	8	30	70
Garden News (W)	2,775	3,960	126*	1	56	44	42	14	37	49	28	72
Shoot (W)	945	1,480	130	1	80	20	16	69	26	5	33	67
No. 1 (W)	1,300	2,250	122	1	42	58	12	90	8	2	40	60
Angling Times (W)	2,490	3,530	115*	1	82	18	14	52	36	12	30	70
Celebrity (W)	1,250	1,875	125	0.5	31	69	51	55	24	21	36	64

Sources: NRS Jan–Dec 1986   ABC Jul–Dec 1986   *ABC Jan–Dec 1986

news and important local events, and with the exception of the sports section, the rest present local news and events. Again, a local organisation can use these to contribute to its publicity activities through both advertising and PR.

Local weekly papers
Most towns have their own local papers which are published once a week. Many of these go back to the nineteenth century and have over the years become an important feature of British town life. Their content covers the news and events of the locality including the local industries, politics, sport and happenings, most of which occur within the boundaries of the circulation areas.

It is fair to assume that the local press covers very broad sections of the community, with a bias towards women, older age groups and often lower income groups. However, we see the emergence in many local papers of children's sections, thus broadening readership to include all but the very young. There is something for everyone in the local press and this is no accident, for editors have long seen the need to produce a publication of interest to the whole community.

For this reason, the contributions made by the local organisations are respected, and a valuable source of information.

The local press allows businesses to advertise in different ways: by using the classified columns, the semi-display areas (such as in the entertainments page) or impactful display space for major advertising campaigns.

Details of all press media regarding coverage, cost and locality can be found in *British Rate and Data – BRAD –* which can be found in most libraries. *BRAD* is the bible for the press media planner.

The press, then, provide opportunities to target towards almost any audience required. Its disadvantages (*vis à vis* TV) lie mainly in the perceived impact of advertising and in many cases the relatively slow build-up of campaigns. Press does, however, present the small business with the ability to reach local and national target audiences with a relatively low cash outlay. Deals can be done with the press, particularly with special interest magazines and local papers, to match editorial space to advertising and to do shared promotional activities. Special interest and local press can be and often are the principal media used by small firms. It is worth your while therefore getting to know the advertising managers and editors of these media well – you will be suprised at the deals you can get.

Radio

From an advertiser's point of view, one of the most significant factors to take into account is that while most adults listen to the radio at some time or another BBC is listened to more often than commercial radio.

There are 45 commercial stations in the UK but whereas some stations such as Radio Piccadilly in Manchester, Clyde in Glasgow, Capital in London and Trent in Nottingham have high local strength it is considered difficult to reach more than 40 per cent of all adults through commercial radio.

Commercial radio audiences have a similar class profile to that of TV, ie down-market with a strong bias towards C2DEs though its age profile is considerably younger. The high quantity of broadcast pop music demonstrates bias towards the younger listener.

Radio advertising can be useful in picking up specific audiences. Between 9.30 and 4.30 pm listenership is heavily biased towards housewives. In the early morning and late afternoon (drive time) a much larger proportion of listeners are working men who tune in while travelling to and from work. From early evening onwards programming is aimed at teenagers and young adults.

The advantages of commercial radio to the small business is that it is relatively cost-efficient and can be targeted quite accurately. While an advertiser trying to reach a national audience may be restricted by absolute coverage levels, a local concern may well find that a combination of commercial radio and local press will provide a strong local campaign. Many of the commercial stations have first-class advertising departments and their representatives will visit you on request and help you plan your campaign. Once again there are lots of deals you can do with your local radio station.

Cinema

There are 600 cinemas in the UK. Two-thirds of all adults never go to the cinema and less than a quarter make more than two visits a year. Cinema should not be discounted as an advertising medium because, unlike any other medium taken as a whole, it has a strong bias towards young ABC1 men – a group which does not watch too much TV. Fifty-six per cent of 15–24 year olds go to the cinema at least twice a year. While not providing main coverage it is a relatively low cost way to advertise locally. Most cinema chains offer a service to local advertisers using standard commercials for a whole range of local services. Deals and local promotions may be available. You can sometimes use the foyers of local cinemas to put up small exhibitions. Again, see your local cinema for details of available opportunities.

Cinemas

No of sites in UK	No of screens in UK	Average weekly admissions
660	1,260	1.39m

Frequency of cinema-going

	Once per month or more	Less than once per month but at least twice per year	Less than twice per year	Never
	%	%	%	%
All adults	6	17	12	65
15–24	21	39	12	28

Profile of average audience

Sex	%	Age	%	Class	%
		15–24	59		
Women	46	25–34	19	ABC1	58
Men	54	35–44	13	C2DE	42
		45+	9		

By permission of Ray Morgan and Partners

Posters

These provide an effective 'do-it-yourself' medium if good sites can be found. Even today, a good hand-produced or simple screen-printed poster can be extremely useful for promoting sales, special offers and so forth and for reinforcing a message in a campaign.

In the latter context posters provide excellent support media. Organisations can often find good, free sites if they take the trouble to look; for example, building society windows, town halls, schools, shop windows and inside factories.

The placing of posters should be planned to gain the maximum possible attention, and if they are in limited supply, attempts to obtain good sites in well-frequented streets should be a priority. (Warning: there are penalties for fly posting, so ensure permission is gained.)

Poster sites can be rented from site owners who will provide not only rates but a lot of information about the potential effectiveness in the areas you choose.

However, it is often difficult to buy precise sites and contracts tend to be for fairly long periods. Poster sites can also be rented on transport, at stations, on parking meters and in theatres.

Posters tend to be an unselective medium in that a conventional poster site is designed to be seen by everyone who passes it, regardless of their age, sex or class. There are, however, exceptions to this: for example a poster site in a shopping centre should reach a proportionately larger number of housewives.

Direct mail

The term 'direct mail' is applied to the use of post as a medium for sending letters and other publicity material to a target audience.

Mail has a number of advantages in that through the availability of good mailing lists it is a highly targetable medium. Direct mail can be turned on or off as required, and it is easy to cost.

As a 'do-it-yourself' medium, letters can be very effective, especially if the organisation can provide itself with adequate lists and do in-house mailing. This medium is covered more fully in Chapter 7 on Direct Response Advertising.

Media for the local business

The small local business in many cases may find that mainstream media may be out of reach. Local press and commercial radio may well meet the needs of most businesses advertising to a local audience. There are, however, a number of minor media that can be employed at very low cost. These might be used to supplement campaigns or for the very small business as the only means of advertising.

Postcards

Postcards carrying a short message, displayed in shop windows, are a very useful medium. For a few pence a week you can place an advertisement. This amazingly cheap form of advertising should not be under-estimated. Many a central heating company or double glazing franchise has got off to a start from leads generated through this medium.

Test different messages to find the one which generates most enquiries. Remember also to renew and change cards regularly and use *coloured card*.

Leaflets

Although an extremely valuable form of communication, leaflets usually turn out to be the least cost-effective method of communication for organisations. The reasons are rarely the fault of the medium itself, but point to a general lack of objectiveness by the organisation. Leaving aside wastage, caused through bad handling and storage (this has been covered in Chapter 6), there are two basic causes of low cost-effective use of leaflets.

First, many leaflets are produced with a total disregard for the purpose for which they are intended. For example, general information leaflets are sent out when a sales message is required, or expensively produced leaflets are handed out at random when a less expensive handbill would be more cost-effective.

Second, enthusiastic publicists, having said 'Let's produce a leaflet', are reluctant to see them being used. They always seem to want to put off the day when they see their coveted supplies being diminished. One day they wake up and find their leaflets out of date, and as a result the money spent on them is a complete waste.

Leaflets can be used as a public relations medium, an advertisement or data sheet. General information leaflets or educational leaflets fall into the public relations category, and leaflets advertising facilities or demanding some form of action on behalf of the reader can be termed as advertising or sales aids.

Leaflets can usually be better employed as support media by placing them in shops, libraries, colleges etc, as an information service or to follow up enquiries from members of the public. Leaflets are also useful in sales interviews and should be left with buyers as 'leave pieces' or reminders.

Shop window displays

Shop windows are a very good place to display your products. Shoppers wandering through a high street find them interesting, stopping to look at items which catch their attention. Get your products displayed in your customers' shop windows. If you own a shop pay particular attention to the quality of your display. Some larger shops will actually rent out display space in their windows at a set rate.

Building societies sometimes have displays of local crafts or industries in their windows. If you have a gallery or craft business you should try to persuade one of the many high street societies to let you display your wares.

Giveaways

There is a whole industry devoted to making and vending giveaways with a sales message to companies. It is all too easy to spend too great a proportion of your budget on calendars, pens, T-shirts and the like. There are some advantages, however, for the small business in leaving pens and calendars with their customers. These serve as reminders but little else. It is difficult to use a giveaway to communicate product benefits. The golden rules with giveaways are:

- promote your product not your company
- give them only to people who are useful to your business
- try always to put your phone number on the item.

For the small business with little to spend on promotion, giveaways should be low on the list of priorities. This does not, however, exclude the possibility of obtaining giveaways from suppliers upon which you can stencil your own company name. Get as many such items as you can – they give you free publicity.

Directories

Yellow Pages and Thomson Local are the two important directories in which every organisation should be listed. Display advertising in these directories will create leads and new customers.

Public speaking

Research has shown that personal recommendation and the passing on of favourable comments by word of mouth are often as powerful a means of recruiting customers as direct advertising. In planning a publicity campaign this point might well be remembered. Every employee, including yourself, is an ambassador for your organisation, at work, at home, on courses or with friends. The spoken word can be used to persuade and communicate through public speaking. In planning effective publicity you would do well to give this form of communication some thought.

It might be useful for you to buy or borrow one or two books on public speaking, if only to improve your own personal ability to communicate; for example, *How to Overcome Nervous Tension and Speak Well in Public*, by Alfred Tack (World Work Limited).

The opportunities to persuade 'captive' audiences about your business and its products are valuable and your shyness or modesty should not let you miss them.

The impression you create at such opportunities will not only help you build your organisation's reputation in the community, it will help too with your own standing and all it will cost you is your time.

Making a media plan

The secret of success in media planning is to reach your target market. So much of the time and effort expended on developing and researching the creative side of advertising will be wasted if it is not delivered to the right audience.

When producing a media plan you will need to take a number of factors into consideration, namely:

- the budget, ie the funds required to finance a campaign
- the target audience, its character and profile
- the geographical coverage of the campaign
- any special creative requirements in terms of displaying or dramatising products being advertised
- three message objectives; what is the purpose – awareness, knowledge or sales?
- the competition – how do they advertise, what media do they use?
- the timing: when and for how long will the campaign be run – are there critical times to coincide with, eg first day of summer sale?
- information – what information is available to help your decisions in what media to use?

The different ways that media planning can be put into practice are:

- use an advertising agency
- use a media independent
- use the media
- do the planning yourself.

Advertising agency

The pros and cons of using an advertising agency are discussed on pages 157-8. The agency, and by this we mean the traditional full service agency, will be able to bring considerable expertise to your entire advertising and marketing as well as to your media planning. Professional planners will provide clients with a high degree of skilled media planning. For this the media will probably pay around 15 per cent commission to the agency on all space booked – smaller accounts may be charged a further fee by the agency.

Media independents

Media independents are mostly based around London. Unlike full service agencies they do one job and that is to plan and buy media.

Media independents will charge between 4 and 7½ per cent commission as a rule. However, rates of commission can be negotiated for expenditure in the region of £50,000 or more. Whereas media independents do not have the creative facilities of a full service agency they can usually recommend design houses, film makers, recording studios, poster designers and so forth to clients. This use of contractors does give the client a choice of services which may help to keep down costs. Media independents also have the ability to negotiate good discounts with the media because of the huge amounts of advertising they place on behalf of clients.

Planning media yourself
Many small businesses with comparatively small advertising budgets are quite successful at media planning. The trick is to keep the plan simple and to concentrate advertising through as few media as possible. Think out the sort of media likely to be available to you and then find out as much about them as possible. Send for rate cards and ask for any information that each publication, radio, TV station has about its audiences – most have research-based information with which they sell their space to advertisers. By working out the size of the audiences you could reach through various publications, you can begin to calculate what you can afford. Remember that it will be necessary to repeat your advertisement several times before you get an effective response, so you will need to multiply the cost of each insertion of your advertisement by the number of times you intend to advertise.

Economics of advertising
Chapter 10 described how publicity should be used to produce a return on the money employed; this cannot be emphasised enough when spending money on advertising. Advertising is expensive, and every penny should be used to maximum effect. Remember, too, that it costs about the same to run an unsuccessful campaign as a successful one.

Bearing in mind that a common reason for the failure of advertising campaigns is that too little money is spent, and for too short a period of time in the right place, how do you ensure from the outset that you are going to spend your money to the best effect?

The key to the problem is to plan your campaign to reach your target audience at the lowest possible cost. For a start you could compare the cost of different publications or other media. The media planner does this by calculating the cost of reaching 1000 target readers (this is known as a 'cost per thousand comparison'). This is quite simple when comparing publications because most of them provide circulation figures. These show you how many papers are printed on average per edition, and you can make an adequate circulation to find the total number of readers by taking the circulation figure and deducting 5 per cent (to cover fluctuations and over-printing) and then multiplying the resulting figure by 2½ (approximate number of readers per copy); this will give you a very approximate idea of readership, eg:

Local newspaper circulation = 12,630
Less 5 per cent = 12,000
Multiply by 2½ = 30,000 readers
  The result equals READERSHIP

In working out the cost per thousand, divide the cost of your advertisement by the readership figure, that is:

Readership = 30,000
Cost of advertisement = £30
Cost per 1000 = £1

You might then apply this principle to papers in your area and discover which is the most competitive. You must be careful, however, not to distort your results by not taking into consideration the number of people you wish to reach. For example, you might have a choice between two papers. One paper has a readership of 15,000 and the advertisement space costs £30; the other only has a circulation of 10,000 and the cost is £25. If the lower readership figure will be sufficient for the campaign then it should be used, even though a cost per thousand comparison would show it to cost more.

Press information

The national press provides readership information to advertisers on request. Unfortunately, this does not always apply to the local press, although their advertising managers can usually be very helpful.

For more detailed information, *British Rate and Data* is indispensable and you would do well to keep a copy handy when planning a campaign. *BRAD* is generally available in most libraries.

From *BRAD* you can glean information regarding circulation, advertising rates, series discounts, mechanical data and the telephone numbers of the advertising managers. *BRAD* also provides a useful mailing list for news releases etc, as it lists every publication in Britain.

Posters
The problem becomes more difficult if we try to compare posters with newspapers. If you are paying for prime sites in the town you might be able to get an idea from the site owner, but if you have managed to obtain free sites, how do you work out their value? Other than by standing at each site for an hour or so and counting everybody who passes by it, there is no way. You do, however, know how much your posters are going to cost. You can view this cost against the work and uncertainty of gaining sufficient coverage as well as against the relative costs of other media and the difficulty of responding.

Direct mail
Direct mail is by far the easiest to calculate with certainty because you know how many letters you are going to send and how much they will cost. (See page 94 for Royal Mail facilities.)

Use local press
We have already talked about the need to reach your target audience in order to expose your message to the maximum number of people with a propensity to take the desired course of action. If your target audience represents a large section of the community, such as a campaign aimed at women generally, then you can straight away see the benefit of using a medium such as the local press. It can only be emphasised that many organisations already value their advertising in it. In fact, much of the work involved in producing posters etc can be avoided by using this local medium to the full.

Weight of advertising
Your campaign must have sufficient weight to be effective; that is, your advertisement must appear with sufficient frequency to make an impression on the target audience and compete for their attention and action, not only with other advertisements but with the other draws on their time. In planning a campaign which will have sufficient weight, you must be conscious of your need to reach your audience with enough impact to attract attention, and often enough to gain a profitable response.

There is no magical formula which allows the media planner to press the right buttons to obtain instant success, but there are three basic requirements for structuring a campaign: coverage, impact and frequency.

Coverage represents the number of people in a given area who will receive its message, in relation to the total audience of the area in which you are going to advertise.

Impact represents the degree to which you can dominate your medium and compete for the attention of the reader. This will take into account both the size of the advertisement and the creative treatment; see Chapter 7.

Frequency is the number of times you will show the audience your advertisement, bearing in mind that you might have to expose your message several times before any impression is made.

Getting the right balance between coverage, impact and frequency will probably demand some tradeoffs when it comes down to practicalities and funds available.

Determining the weight of the campaign

The weight of the campaign depends almost entirely on the sums of money spent upon it, although 'free advertising' techniques can be applied to supplement them. This naturally begs the question: what should be spent on the campaign? In Chapter 10 we looked at the need to plan expenditure against the return, but we can now go further; we can look at our objectives more closely. What are they in precise terms?

While there is not a book on the market that will tell you exactly how much to spend on any campaign, you can draw some lessons from the professional planner, who might work out what to spend on achieving their objectives based on:

- experience
- comparing other people's advertising
- using a step-by-step execution of a campaign
- using the overkill method.

Experience
The advertiser in big industry can call on years of experience and, often by looking at a task, can make a realistic judgement of his requirements. Eventually, I hope that the reader will find himself in this

position. The secret is to keep good records of every activity undertaken – a lot of companies keep records of responses to advertising on computer, enabling them to analyse the effectiveness of each advertisement and each publication used.

Comparing other people's advertising
Local firms, shops and other organisations are probably advertising. It is worth talking to some of the people already engaged in local advertising. Established advertising departments can sometimes be very helpful and may well be able to give advice on choice of media and the weight of the campaign. One good idea is to watch out for specific campaigns by other organisations and then to make enquiries to find out how cost-effective they were. Some firms are reluctant to give out information; others will be extremely helpful.

The advertising manager of the local paper may also be able to cite examples of campaigns to help you (but remember advertising managers are paid to sell space).

Step-by-step campaign
One very useful bit of advice during your early experiences with advertising is to *start out small and grow big*. Run campaigns first of all in your locality or in those special interest publications read by people interested in your product. As you become more successful and have gained experience you can gradually expand your campaigns. Some of your early lessons in media buying might prove expensive so caution, evaluation of information and a step-by-step approach might help you to gain the necessary experience and feel for your campaigns, without too many mishaps. Furthermore it allows you to build up responses to a manageable level. (See direct response advertising, Chapter 7, pages 77-94).

Overkill method
This term is used to describe the practice of deliberately committing a greater weight of advertising than is required to achieve objectives. The application of this practice can often ensure success. The danger is in spending too much, and adversely affecting the profitability of the campaign. However, as opposed to spending too little on vital operations, this practice is sometimes preferable.

The low-budget advertiser can and should support his campaign with free advertising, where possible, to help increase the weight of delivery and ensure that the campaign is successful.

Concentration of resources

One of the prime errors in producing an advertising campaign is to spend vital funds on too many media. Your campaign will be more likely to achieve the best results by concentrating energies into as few media as possible. For example, an organisation with £4000 to spend will see better results by spending all the money in the local press, rather than by using the money buying some posters, some leaflets and then only taking a few advertisements in the press.

The reasons for concentrating your resources are:

1. You can maintain a more structured campaign optimising your coverage, frequency and maximising impact.
2. You are committing as little as possible to creative and production costs; that is, you are spending more on delivering the message.
3. You reduce the amount of administration work, which means you can spend more time on doing one job adequately.

Gaining momentum in a continuous advertising campaign

When you are building up a continuous campaign, you could compare it with riding a bicycle. With the same pressure on the pedals you go faster and faster; in other words, you build up momentum. Pundits in the advertising world believe that momentum can be built up in advertising; that is, by maintaining continuous advertising pressure, you can build up its effective weight at an increasing rate. Leading from this hypothesis comes the view that, rather than relying on continuous pressure, you can find a way of reducing your expenditure by running your advertising in spaced bursts. The burst effect has numerous advantages, both from the point of view that it maintains momentum (provided that the gap between each burst is not too long) and might lead to some cost savings, so that we can increase the duration of the campaign.

The latter point can be of great benefit when your campaign is supporting continuous promotional activity or when you have a prolonged educational campaign. Examples are shown in Figures 11.1 and 11.2. In Figure 11.2 the duration of the campaign is extended and although you might expect the peak response to come slightly later, you do have the benefit of maintaining advertising activity for a longer period. However, you will need to run your initial burst long enough for your campaign to register with your target audience.

Media Planning 151

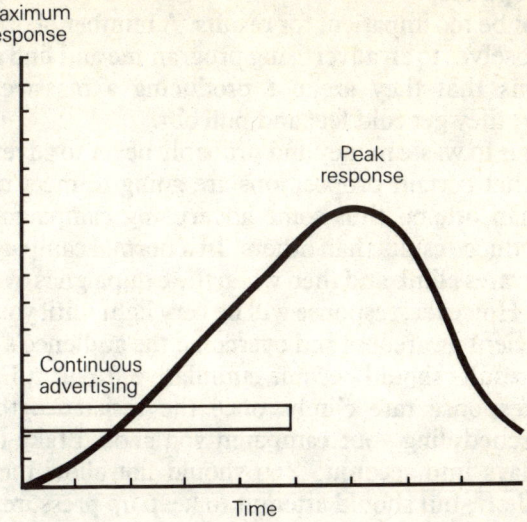

Figure 11.1 *Continuous advertising — response pattern*

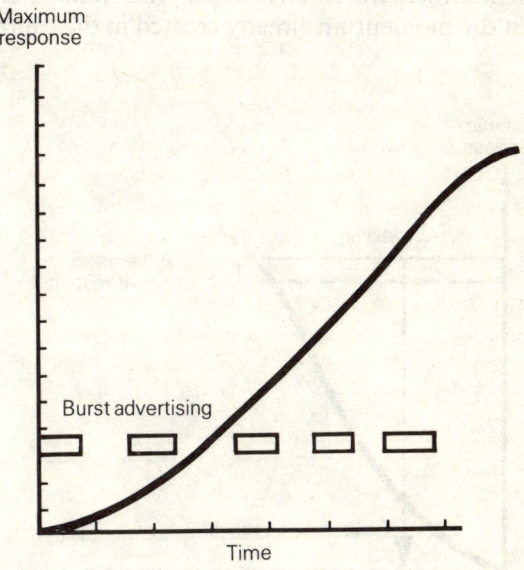

Figure 11.2 *Burst advertising — response pattern*

Delays in response

You must not be too impatient for results. A number of organisations commit themselves to an advertising programme and find after only a few insertions that they are not producing a massive response. Immediately, they get cold feet and pull out.

The result is to waste money and probably never to advertise again. Remember that certain propositions are going to meet more initial resistance than others, thus some advertising campaigns will take longer to produce results than others. In a normal campaign you will see response rates climb and then when the campaign is over they will begin to fall. However, response will be very light until you have both created sufficient awareness and overcome the audience's resistance. Thereafter, results should become cumulative. Look at Figure 11.3. Note how response rate climbs once the resistance threshold is broken. In scheduling your campaign you should take this idea of response delays into account. You should not allow the campaign simply to tail off, but should attempt to keep up pressure for as long as possible, because the peak response may not be forthcoming until the later stages of the campaign. Under no account is it advisable to let the campaign dribble away with the occasional insertion here and there as response rates may as a result begin to decay prematurely. Each advertisement should be strategically inserted in an effort to capitalise upon the momentum already created in the campaign.

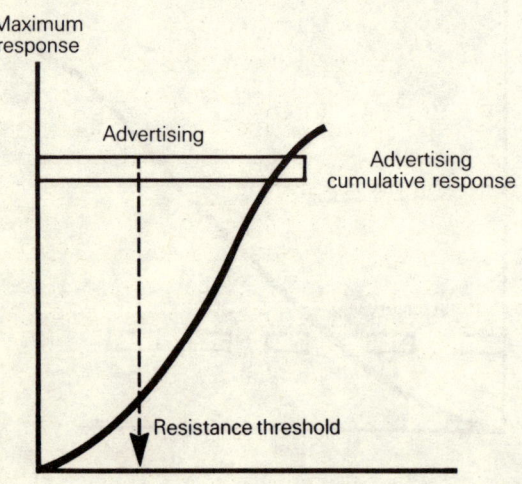

Figure 11.3 *Delays in response*

Coding advertisements

In order to tell which publications produce the best results, you should code reply coupons in such a way as to allow you to sort and analyse replies by publication. Normally the press would do this as a matter of course at the end of a campaign; you can then analyse the results to find the relative effectiveness of each publication and use this formation to help plan future campaigns.

Here you can use your personal computer to store information to calculate such vital pieces of information as:

- Which forms of media or publicaton achieve the highest response, including such information as position, page and advertisement size
- What proportion of respondents become customers
- How long is the normal response pattern between publishing and advertisement and receiving enquiries?
- The proportion of respondents generated by advertising versus personal recommendation etc, and further analysed to differentiate between leads and actual sales.

Buying space

Having made your plan, the next stage is to buy the space. (We shall deal only with buying press space, as this is the most complex and probably the most commonly used medium by the organisations for which this book is written.)

Units of purchase

You might, at this stage, pick up a newspaper within easy reach and look at how pages are printed. You will see that the material is arranged in columns, and the purchase of space is governed by these (the columns, incidentally, vary in size from one publication to another). The units of purchase are single-column centimetres; that is, one centimetre depth of a single-column width. The publication's advertising rate-card will give the cost per single-column centimetre, and the calculation of a total price for the space can be worked out by multiplying the cost of a single-column centimetre by the total number of column centimetres the advertisement will occupy.

However, certain publications may well have individual rates for say a whole page, half-page, quarter-page etc which show a saving on the column centimetres calculation. This is a deliberate policy to encourage advertisers to buy larger spaces.

Measuring the advertisement

When placing an order for an advertisement, the space should be booked by giving the publication the size (length first and number of columns second). For example, 20 centimetres across two will give you an advertisement 20 centimetres deep, two columns wide. (This also applies when briefing designers.)

Choice of position – display space

The least expensive way of buying display space is to ask for 'run of paper rate' which implies that you are not fussy where your advertisement is placed in the publication. For this you will receive a sizeable saving. If, however, you wish to ensure the competitiveness of the advertisement, you might ask for a solus space – that is, your advertisement is all on its own on a page – or you might ask for it to be facing matter, that is, facing editorial and not next to someone else's advertisement.

If you buy a page you might choose it to be on the right-hand side, which is supposedly better read that the left-hand side, or you might even specify a front or back page. For all these you will be paying anything from 20 to 100 per cent more than for the 'run of paper'. Most advertisers generally prefer to buy 'run of paper' and, by buying space well ahead, it is usually possible to get good space. If, however, the publication chosen happens to be one of those which appears to consist mainly of advertisements, then precise space-buying might be worth the extra cost. Also, if you want to run a high-impact campaign on the opening day of a summer sale, or to get a large attendance at an event, precise buying can ensure the competitiveness that you need. (Note that the TV page is always the best place to advertise.)

Now turn to the classified columns of the paper. Here again you buy in units of single-column centimetres, although you can often buy at a line or word rate. You must always be sure when purchasing classified space that your advertising message will fit into the amount purchased.

Other areas

Some publications sell useful space, say above the title on the front page or in the 'stop press' column; these command premium prices and are usually booked well in advance.

Lead time

One point that should be remembered is that every publication has a deadline for receiving advertisements, and that any material presented after the required time is unlikely to be used. What is more, an organisation, having already booked the space, and being unable to supply its material on time, will become the proud owner of white space. There is no recourse for this, as every paper specifies that all material should be submitted before a certain date. This for a local paper may be a day or two before going to press; for a magazine it could be a couple of months. This period is known as 'lead time'. It is as well to make sure that lead time for all the selected publications is known and it should also be remembered that, if display advertisement material is to be presented in forms other than flat artwork or blocks (see Chapter 5), then additional time is required to allow the publication to make up the advertisement.

Discounts

One of the secrets of getting good value for money in advertising is knowing how and when discounts are applicable. For a start, many publications charge a slightly lower rate for certain types of advertising. Recruitment advertising for a local firm is for example likely to be more costly than advertising an event.

There are also series discounts for taking more than a certain number of insertions. These discounts can to some extent be considered in planning the campaign in order to gain the best value for money, but you must not fundamentally change a well-thought-out plan simply to take advantage of the quantity discount.

There are also combined and group rates for associated publications. For example, a local paper in one town may have an associate company producing for a neighbouring town. In such cases, there will certainly be a substantial discount for advertising in both. In fact, many use common pages, and advertisements taken in these will show a sizeable saving.

Special discounts

A regular advertiser will go on to the publication's client list, and will be advised of special discounts that become available. A good buyer will be on the look-out for these among his chosen publications, and taking advantage of them may present savings. If you beware of frittering money away on every deal that appears, to the detriment of the plan, the occasional special discount can save you money.

Advertorial packages

Special deals can be negotiated for advertorial packages, ie a combination of editorial and advertising. Furthermore, why not get your suppliers to pay for some of the advertising in an advertorial feature?

Stop numbers – cancellation

On occasion you might, for one reason or another, have to cancel an advertisement at short notice. The urgency may demand that the telephone be used. Most publications will cancel the advertisement and issue a stop number to the customer. This is a form of receipt. Should this number be lost and the advertisement still appear, then the publication may attempt to demand payment. The best advice is to ask for and retain the stop number.

Media schedule

Display your media plan on a media schedule, an example of which is illustrated in Figure 11.4. The advantages of doing so are:

- You can see at a glance when each advertisement is due to appear
- Other promotional and PR activities can be overlaid on to the schedule to see how they interact
- Copies of the schedule can be given to salesmen to inform them of the organisation's activities
- The schedule itself makes a good format against which to record results.

Media	April 5	12	19	26	31	May 3	10	17	24	June 7	14	21	28	July 5	12	19	26
Radio spots	3	1	1	1	1												
Evening Post ½ page display	3	2	2	2			5	5			5	5	5				
Boat Owner			1					1				1					
Sunday Times Classified			1				1	1			1						
	New showroom opens					Exhibition				Sales drive South coast							

Figure 11.4 *A simple media schedule*

CHAPTER 12
Selecting an Advertising Agency

Once an organisation is ready to start advertising on a large scale it really does need an advertising agency. By an advertising agency we are talking about a full service agency which not only creates advertising and buys media, but provides a variety of other service options as well, such as sales promotion, print design, marketing planning, research and so on. The benefits that a competent agency are likely to bring to the organisation are:

- Planning advertising campaigns
- Creating and designing advertisements
- Selecting and buying media space
- Producing finished artwork and commercials
- Researching and evaluating campaigns
- Advising on marketing options.

Although a number of these functions could be undertaken in-house for all but the very small business reliant upon limited advertising, an advertising agency can make a sizeable contribution to the effective running of a business. The advantage of using an agency is that a much higher degree of professionalism can be focused on the organisation's advertising in terms of meeting marketing objectives, planning campaigns, creating advertising and buying space in the media. A reasonably talented agency should be able to offer the following, even to a fairly modest advertiser:

- Expertise in marketing and advertising
- Creativity in presenting and promoting products
- Buying power with the media that ensures that even a small client can buy at the agency's best rates
- Independent advice, thus providing wisdom and counsel to the people running the organisation

- Quality of design and presentation beyond anything that can normally be planned in-house.

Yet while advertising agencies compete strongly for large consumer product accounts with multi-million pound budgets, it would astound many entrepreneurs to know how much money agencies can actually get through in making films, directing and producing, artworks or even roughs. The fact that Wimbledon and Ascot are times when clients have hospitality lavished upon them by leading agencies indicates that large sums are involved and shows the importance agencies place upon excellent client relations.

So, for the small business how is a suitable agency found? First, unless there is something really special about the business or product, steer clear of the big agencies. Use a smaller provincial agency which will probably be a full service publicity company which may also offer, apart from just advertising, PR facilities and sales promotion. You may have the opportunity to make a selection in your own town, but there is no need, other than from a convenience point of view, to employ an agency in your town or city.

The selection process

The steps involved in the search and selection of an agency might be summarised as follows:

Step 1
Analyse your own business and the way it is set up. Ask yourself who is going to make the advertising decision as this will be important in ensuring good chemistry exists between the chosen person and the agency account team.

Step 2
Write a brief to be sent to agencies you feel can handle your business. The brief should include a description of:

- The company and how it came into being
- The products and any special features that make it unique
- The market and the position the organisation occupies in the market
- An idea of what is expected from the agency.

Step 3
Draw up a list of candidates that can be shortlisted. Finding grounds

upon which to select is difficult but the following might help:
- Look for material produced by the candidate agencies and see if you can get a feel for their work
- Ask around, talk to advertisers in similar sized businesses to yours and get some names.
- Selection of services are available, eg Advertising Agency Register, 62 Shaftesbury Avenue, London, W1V 7DE; but these are largely concerned with 'big client' needs.
- Directories such as the 'Blue Book' (*Advertisers Annual*) list agencies and clients but again these tend to be more useful for the big client.

Step 4

Go out and meet advertising agencies, if you have never met one before. The more you visit, the more you will get to know what they offer and how they operate. Use this step to learn about advertising agencies as well as to get a feel for the type of people with whom you could best get along and who are going to provide a good service. Some agencies may decline to handle your work because there may be a conflict with another client or simply because you are not going to spend enough to make it worthwhile for them to offer much of a service. Agency people are generally very sympathetic to a business with obvious potential (a future big spender) and if they cannot themselves help, they may be able to find another suitable agency which will offer to take on your business.

During this step, it's quite a good idea to get agencies to show you their work and explain what they have done for their existing clients. Very often the agency has a standard presentation which shows their performance in terms of client work and the size of the billings (the total value of advertising placed on behalf of clients). This should be rising if the agency is any good. Look also at the size of their client accounts; will yours be a sprat or a whale? Look too to see if the agency is dominated by a single major account; if so there is every likelihood that anybody who is any good in the agency will be tied up with it.

Step 5

This is the time to make a shortlist of all the agencies. Try to get the number down to three. Here the hard work of selection has to rest upon the presentation by the agencies to you, the potential client, and this might be based upon:

- how you think you can work with the agency
- what you think of their advertising
- how best they seem to respond to the goals you set in your original briefing.

If your account is really quite small then you may not be in a position to choose from too many candidates, in which case go for a newly set up agency hungry for clients – but make sure of the agency people's experience and client base first as *you* might end up having to advise *them*.

Step 6
You might be able to persuade the agency to outline some creative proposals for your business, and also to suggest how they would plan the media for the advertising they have created for you. At one time agencies would often do a presentation for virtually nothing and some of the newer hungry ones still do. For the small client an informal assessment of the task may be all that the agency will be prepared to do for free. Obviously, any one of your candidates that bends over backwards to win the account has to be a front runner, given that what is produced is reasonably good.

Step 7
This is the step when you make the final decision and your judgement will be based on your opinions of the people, past work and the presentations the agency has done for you.

From experience I would suggest that you select any agency which:

- grasps what you understand by the market in which your product competes;
- shows at least a superficial understanding of the products to be advertised;
- has some ideas that you find workable and attractive;
- has the will and capacity to produce good advertising for your products;
- has the intention of giving you good service regardless of the size of your potential billing;
- has people with whom you know you can get along.

Paying the agency

The most commonly adopted system for paying advertising agencies is for them to take a commission from the media on space that they buy on a client's behalf. For large advertisers the average rate is about 15 per cent. Agencies prefer, however, to work on a fee basis for their clients and this is becoming a trend. For the smaller client a mixture of fees and commission may be required, but this is by no means a set rule and ultimately it will be a matter for negotiation.

Specialist advertising agencies will charge fees, as will those providing services such as market research, sales promotion, print design, and so forth, for such work done on behalf of a client. Advertising agencies are used to handling and spending large sums of money so make sure you keep a tight grip on your budget and ensure that the agency knows the limit of your expenditure.

CHAPTER 13
Choosing a PR Consultancy

The need for a PR consultancy usually becomes apparent when either organisation has a major PR exercise to do such as getting an Unlisted Securities Market issue off the ground, when it requires backers, or when it is under attack. Most small businesses manage quite well without consultancies and if there is someone within the organisation who is good at PR it may be premature even to consider using a consultancy.

It is worth noting that more and more companies are turning to PR consultants. PR meets communications needs recognised by both large and small companies. Good professional advice from a consultant can go a long way to producing a low-cost but effective means of reaching target interest groups.

The PR agency can bring to the organisation:

- Professional skills and event organisational ability
- Influential contacts in the media
- News story creation and writing expertise
- Access to support facilities such as video making, exhibition stand designers etc
- Advice on public relations and company image developments.

The selection process

Steps in finding and selecting a PR consultancy are as follows:

Step 1
Decide why a consultancy is needed. Is it for a special assignment, to provide ongoing activities such as the launch of a new product? It is essential that you know why and what is wanted from a consultancy before going to the trouble of seeking one.

Choosing a PR Consultancy

Step 2
Find the right sort of consultancy to meet the organisation's needs. There are a number of ways of finding candidates and probably the best is from personal recommendations, given that whoever is recommending is in a position to advise rather than just get the job for friends.

There are a number of organisations to which PR companies either belong, have professional alliances with, or to which they subscribe:

- The Incorporated Society of British Advertisers
- The Public Relations Consultants Association
- The Institute of Public Relations
- Advertising agencies.

Step 3
Decide on the type of consultancy that would be best for you. This will reflect your requirements – will you require a full-service consultancy, ie one that tackles every aspect of PR, a financial PR consultancy, or a specialist one? Ideally a small hungry local consultancy would probably be best suited to the smaller business requiring a full PR service.

Step 4
Draw up a list of candidates of, say, not more than six PR consultancies and send them a description of the organisation, its products and outline your objectives and requirements.

Step 5
Visit the consultancies that show interest and use each visit as an experience-gaining exercise. Discuss your PR requirement face-to-face with the consultants. Get a feel for consultants and the way in which they approach their business. Use this stage to find people who are both competent and whom you can get along with.

Step 6
As with finding an advertising agency, reduce the candidate consultancies to about two or three and ask them to make proposals for handling your business and outline what they believe your communication needs are. There may or may not be a fee involved (usually not) for a presentation as most consultancies will not go to the depth of detail and creativity that one might expect from an advertising agency presentation.

Try and evolve a number of meetings with candidate consultancies. This will help you to get to know their people and also allow you to get under their gloss.

Step 7
Now is the time to talk over remuneration. PR consultancies charge fees and these will be related to the level of service that they will be contracted to carry out. There is no reason why the small business or organisation cannot use a PR consultancy on a limited part-time basis – provided the consultancy is willing to go along with the idea.

Step 8
Agree methods by which the effectiveness of the PR generated can be evaluated. Obviously this needs to relate to both the quantity and quality of editorial achieved but more importantly on the effect the editorial has on target interest groups.

Step 9
Appoint the consultancy with a contract which includes services expected, fees and termination clauses.

CHAPTER 14
Planning Your Promotional Activities

This final chapter puts into context all that has gone before. In the preceding chapters the various techniques and ideas for creating promotion have been examined. Each technique presents an alternative answer to a particular promotional problem, yet using them piecemeal without thinking out what is, or needs to be, achieved will not enable you to use your knowledge to maximum effect. No general would envisage fighting a battle by sending in one man at a time. So with promotion you will need to orchestrate your activities to maximise the amount of promotional and PR communications that will hit the market. At the same time you will need to know what objectives you are aiming for and how much money you can afford for your campaigns.

Each element of your promotional plan should have its own set of objectives, for example:

- product advertising to stimulate enquiries
- product PR activity directed at the trade to support distribution
- exhibitions to find new distributors
- advertisements to recruit staff
- organisational PR ahead of a USM issue etc.

Each element should be targeted and monitored for effectiveness with adjustment to objectives or activities as and when required.

You might then consider producing your promotional plan for a six- or even a 12-month period, thus developing a total promotional strategy to embrace all your activities.

The promotional plan is constructed by looking at the organisation's total objectives and planning the use of individual techniques to achieve them. Yet you cannot take the 'ivory tower' route; a theoretically plausible plan might sound all right on paper, but it must be totally realistic to be achievable. The objectives themselves need to be attainable, the plan needs to be costed and there must be adequate resources available to carry it out.

The two biggest costs of a promotional programme are *time* and *money*. The more you do yourself the greater the amount of time you will need to devote to it. In making your plan therefore allocate your time carefully. Things will begin to break down if you overstretch yourself and have no reserves of time to put right things that go wrong. The hours spent on getting a publicity plan together will be wasted if you cannot spend enough time on the execution. This point is important.

Above all the financial side of the plan must be both well-planned and controlled. Do not over-extend the organisation's financial resources, because if the payback takes longer than planned the organisation may end up with more problems than it started with. The aim of promotion is to increase the wealth and market standing of the organisation. A poor financial situation usually means that your efforts have to be diverted to the endless race to raise enough cash to meet next month's bills. The organisation that sees effective promotional activity as a means of coping with an already poor financial situation should not gamble its last few pounds on a 'make-or-break' type of operation, but should look more objectively at its problems. Having done so, it will identify its key problems and set its priority objectives to solving them. Then by taking its time it might cautiously proceed on a limited promotional programme, gently easing the situation. None of the operations should present the remotest possibility of exacerbating the organisation's problems.

The key, then, to producing effective promotion is to identify and set objectives to be achieved over a period of time by a well-planned and integrated promotional plan.

Put the plan down on paper

If you take the time to look at your publicity goals objectively, you will see there are a great number of advantages in planning activities well in advance. This makes them easier to co-ordinate and integrate and allows you to put your ideas into perspective. Monthly or even weekly sessions devoted to trying to think up something to do on the publicity front are rarely effective. You might even compare it to a builder trying to erect a house without a plan. A plan written to include the outline future promotional activity will not only save time in the long run, but will give you more flexibility to make quick responses to changes in your competitors' activities or to exploit opportunities as they arise.

Have a plan to work to and set projects within it that can be built up. Obviously, the plan will have to revolve around major events such as exhibitions, sales promotions and new line launches. By careful planning you can focus promotion on to the business at these times to ensure maximum exposure when the organisation most wants to seek customer and trade support.

The plan should be written. Not only will it act as a working reference and checklist but it will also serve as a record of what is intended; and do not forget, you might for a variety of reasons find yourself out of circulation for a while – thus the plan will allow someone else to carry on.

The previous chapters cover in some detail different aspects of promotional techniques and ideas that could be introduced into a plan.

The following section has been produced as a working template for the construction of a publicity plan. Read through it and answer the questions posed; by so doing, you should end up with a publicity plan. The actual writing of the plan could be little more than reasoned headings based upon your answers.

Five stages to mounting the promotional programme

Stage 1: Analyse what has to be done
1. What do you want to do?
    (a) Promote your products/launch new products?
    (b) Raise finance?
    (c) Win support?
2. What stands in your way?
    (a) Can you identify specific problems?
    (b) What do people think of the organisation?
    (c) Do you need to improve your image?
    (d) Are there groups or factions that generally oppose the existence of the organisation? If so, what reasons do they have?
    (e) Are there competing organisations or interests that are likely to affect the organisation's ability to sell its products, influence the trade and raise finance?

Stage 2: Assess your current situation
3. What strengths and weaknesses does the organisation present?
    (a) Are your aims and aspirations compatible with
        — the size of your maximum potential market?
        — your product range?
        — your customer and logistics support?
        — your relations with your customers?
    (b) Are your resources adequate?
        — Do you have the necessary finance to run your business progressively?
        — Do you have backup sources of funds?
        — Do you have good people with skills?
        — Can you expand production to meet additional demand created by your publicity?
        — Are you going to run the publicity yourself or do you have staff or professional support?
        — Do you have the human resources to run a news release service etc?
        — Do you have any special skills, eg ability to write, illustrate or photograph?
    (c) What about the competitors?
        — What are their strengths and weaknesses?
        — Do any control the distribution trade?
        — Are they bigger, stronger, cheaper etc?
        — What market positions do they hold in relation to your intended position?
        — Do they obtain more PR coverage than you?
        — Do they advertise – if so, where, and how much do they spend?
        — Is their sales force larger or better trained? Does it offer more products etc?
        — How does your customer service compare with your competitors'?
        — Do your competitors have an identifiable and favourable corporate image?

Stage 3: Plan what is going to be done
1. Set objectives
    (a) What are your sales objectives?
    (b) What are your financial objectives?
    (c) What are your opinion-forming objectives?
2. Establish a clear strategy:
    (a) What is your strategy for the period of the programme and how does it relate to the long-term aspirations of the organisation?

(b) Set individual goals for promotional activities, advertising and public relations. How will these work together to make the total plan successful?

Stage 4: Work out the execution of the plan
1. State how the promotions plans will be implemented
   (a) What activities or events will be required to achieve promotional goals?
   (b) When, where and how will the events take place?
2. State how advertising plans will be implemented
   (a) How will advertising be used to support the publicity programme?
   (b) Advertising to support selling, finance-raising, opinion-forming and staff recruitment
   (c) Advertising of events, stunts, exhibitions etc
   (d) Advertising of other sales supporting activities, promotions, sales aids etc
   (e) What media will be used to reach the target audience: press, posters, leaflets, free material etc?
3. State how the public relations plan will support the publicity programme
   (a) Who are your principal target interest groups?
   (b) What do you want them to think about the organisation?
   (c) How will you reach them; for example, news release service to the media, letters, talks, advertising etc?
4. Co-ordination of the plan
   (a) Plan out major activities and events – and tie in support activity so as to provide a continuous, integrated plan. (A visual planner such as a flow chart is a good idea.)
   (b) Nominate individuals to carry out any tasks well ahead of time.
   (c) Ensure that all material is either at hand or will be in time for when it is needed. (Do not forget about lead times.)
   (d) Discuss the financial situation with the accountant and list all items of expenditure and estimate when individual items will have to be paid for – work to the budget and stick to it.
   (e) Circulate copies of the plan to everyone involved and indicate how and when they are involved.

Stage 5: Appraisal of results
Having taken the time, trouble and expense of mounting a publicity programme, many organisations fail to review their achievements.

Very often a great deal of money, time and trouble can be saved in subsequent activities by the objective appraisal of a plan. It is therefore advisable to check results.

1. Ask yourself at regular intervals:
   (a) Are you achieving your planned objectives? If not, what can be done to make the necessary adjustments to the plan to put you back on target?
   (b) Are you ahead of your planned objectives? If so, are you going to exploit the situation or would it be more profitable to reduce the amount of activity and spare valuable funds?
1. (c) What information can you collect and store on your personal computer, eg enquiries from press advertisements?
2. Final assessment of achievements:
   (a) What was the final achievement of the plan? Were all the objectives achieved? If not, to what extent were they missed?
   (b) Were there any specific problems which adversely affected the organisation's ability to run its programme? If so, how were they surmounted and how can they be avoided in future?
   (c) How did the organisation's techniques stand up to the plan?
      — Were promotions, advertising and events successful?
      — Was the news release service effective? (How many cuttings were gained against the number of releases sent out?)
      — Were there any notably successful releases and conversely were there any notably unsuccessful ones?
   (d) The last question is possibly the most important—was the publicity campaign cost-effective?

Aim to get the whole of the organisation involved in creating a highly tuned image for the business, ie make sure that:

- the telephone operator is polite and helpful
- sales staff are prompt and well-informed
- service engineers and after-sales service personnel are polite and caring
- delivery staff are smart and alert.

Then ensure that your letterheadings, reception, company vehicles and so forth reflect a consistent and quality image. All these intentions should become organisation goals. The whole business should hum with the desire to service the customer and project a positive image for the organisation. It won't happen on its own. It won't happen by writing memos. It will demand leadership and dedication, commitment and determination.

Further tips on running your own business

There are just a few more tips worth conveying. Promotion is an excellent weapon with which to lead your attack on the market-place. You should, however, ensure that overall management of your business is adequate to cope with the stresses of expansion. The following need care if you are to run a successful business:

Cash flow
Forecast this well, by avoiding over-estimating sales, under-estimating revenue, under-estimating major costs, keeping up budgeted expenses and revising regularly.

Sales and marketing
Make really sure you understand your market and use your promotional and sales force skills to exploit opportunities and to beat the competition.

Organisation image
Work on the way you appear and behave. Remember *customer service* is your primary image builder.

Costing and pricing
Accurate costing and competitive pricing are essential to business success. Constantly monitor:

- material costs and supplies
- general expenses
- productivity and efficiency.

Budgeting
Set an expenditure budget for your costs, production, sales, profits and cash requirements. Plan in detail for 12 months ahead and prepare outlines for two and five years to the future.

Manage your own skills and those of your staff
First ensure that you can visualise the whole of the business and not

just the area which interests you most. Understand finance and budgeting and be able to sell and negotiate.

Attend courses, seminars, exhibitions and conferences. Read trade and industry literature. Always be ready to seek advice.

Was it worth it?

My hopes are that this book will have stimulated your interest in promotion and will see you through many years of success in the furtherance of the aims and aspirations of your organisation. If you remember, above all, that success is the best motivator, you will gain a great deal from trying out the ideas in this book. Try them on a small scale at first, and then as you gain experience and confidence, go further to bigger and more exciting projects in the future. Promoting your own business can be tremendous fun and will provide you with a new and exciting talent; that of being able to build your business by selling your ideas and motivating everyone involved in your *success*!

Chapter 1: Promoting Your Own Business

REFERENCES
Kotler, P, *Marketing Management*, Prentice Hall International Inc, London 1984
Hart, Norman, *The Director*

KOGAN PAGE TITLE
Successful Marketing for the Small Business, The Daily Telegraph Guide, Dave Patten, 1985

USEFUL INFORMATION
Business Monitor, HMSO
Chambers of Commerce
Current British Directories, CBD Research Ltd
Directory of British Associations, CBD Research Ltd
Frost and Sullivan Reports, Frost and Sullivan, London
Guide to Official Statistics, Government Statistical Office
International Directory of Published Market Research, British Overseas Trade Board
Trade Associations
Trade Press
Who Owns Whom
Yellow Pages

JOURNALS
Campaign
Industrial Marketing Digest
Marketing
Marketing Week

Chapter 2: Advertising

REFERENCE
Roman, Kenneth and Maas, Jane, *How to Advertise*, Kogan Page, 1979

KOGAN PAGE TITLES
Effective Advertising: The Daily Telegraph Guide for the Small Business, H C Carter, 1986

174 *How to Promote Your Own Business*

OTHER READING
Advertising Law, R G Lawson, Macdonald and Evans
The Practice of Advertising, N A Hart and J O'Connor, Heinemann

USEFUL INFORMATION
The Advertising Association
15 Wilton Road
London SW1 1NJ
01-828 2771

Advertising Standards Authority
1 Brook House
2-16 Torrington Place
London WC1E 7HN
01-580 5555

Association of Mail Order Publishers
1 New Burlington Street
London W1X 1FD
01-437 0706

Communication, Advertising and Marketing Foundation Ltd (CAM)
Abford House
15 Wilton Road
London SW1V 1NJ
01-828 7506

Incorporated Society of British Advertisers
44 Hertford Street
London W1Y 8AE
01-499 7502

Chapter 3: Public Relations

REFERENCES
Churchill, David, *Choosing and Using a PR Consultancy: The Director's Guide*, The Director Publications, 1985
Kotler, P, *Marketing Management*, Prentice Hall, London, 1984
National Westminster Bank, *Small Business Digest*, No 22, July 1986

KOGAN PAGE TITLES
Be Your Own PR Man: Practical Public Relations for the Small Business, 2nd edn, Michael Bland, 1987
Effective PR Management: A Guide to Corporate Survival, Paul Winner, 1987
Promoting Yourself on Television and Radio, Michael Bland and Simone Mondesir, 1987
PR Week Marketing and Public Relations Handbook, 1987

OTHER READING
Public Relations Practice, Wilfred Howard (ed), Heinemann

PUBLICATIONS
PR Week

USEFUL INFORMATION
The Institute of Public Relations
Gate House
St John's Square
London EC1M 4DH
01-253 5151

Chapter 4: Sales Promotion, Merchandising, Selling and Exhibiting

REFERENCE
National Westminster Bank, *Small Business Digest*, No 16, January 1986

KOGAN PAGE TITLES
Customer Service: How to Achieve Total Customer Satisfaction, Malcolm Peel, 1987
Do Your Own Market Research, Paul N Hague and Peter Jackson, 1987
Getting Sales: A Practical Guide to Getting More Sales for Your Business, Richard D Smith and Ginger Dick, 1984
A Handbook of Sales and Marketing Management, Len Rogers, 1987
The Industrial Market Research Handbook, 2nd edn, Paul N Hague, 1987
Selling by Telephone: Tested Techniques to Make Every Call Count, Len Rogers, 1986

Successful Marketing for the Small Business: The Daily Telegraph Guide, Dave Patten, 1985

OTHER READING
Sales Promotion in Action, C Petersen, Associated Business Plans

USEFUL INFORMATION
Telemarketing and Consultancy
DEW Marketing
Lynton
Blacksmiths End
Staphern
Melton Mowbray
Leics

COURSES
Institute of Marketing
Moor Hall
Cookham
Maidenhead
Berkshire SL6 9QH
06285 24922

Learning International Ltd
(personal selling skills);
Spenklin House
Gunnersbury Avenue
London W4 5QB
01-994 8592

Chapter 5: Designing Press Advertisements

REFERENCES
Crompton, Alastair, *Craft of Copywriting*, Business Books, 1979
Killough, James A, 'Improved Payoffs', *Harvard Business Review*, July/August 1978

KOGAN PAGE TITLES
How to Advertise, Kenneth Roman and Jane Maas, 1979
Effective Advertising: The Daily Telegraph Guide for the Small Business, H C Carter, 1986

USEFUL INFORMATION
Choosing and Using an Advertising Agency: The Director's Guide, The Director Publications, 1985, for a glossary of terms plus a lot more useful information on advertising agencies
Yellow Pages for names of designers and commercial artists

Chapter 7: Direct Response Advertising

REFERENCES
Direct Marketing: The Director's Guide, Institute of Directors, August 1986
Marketing Week
National Westminster Bank, *Small Business Digest*, No 18, July 1985

KOGAN PAGE TITLES
The Business Guide to Effective Writing, J A Fletcher and D Gowing, 1987
Direct Mail, Principles and Practice, Robin Fairlie, 1979
Readymade Business Letters, Jim Dening, 1986
Running Your Own Mail Order Business, Malcolm Breckman, 1987

OTHER READING
The Mail User's Handbook, M Corby and R Fairlie, BDMA, London
The Post Office Direct Mail Handbook, L Andrews, BDMA, London, 1984

USEFUL ADDRESSES
Association of Mail Order Publishers
1 New Burlington Street
London W1X 1FD
01-437 0706

The British Direct Marketing Association
1 New Oxford Street
London WC1A 1NQ
01-242 2254

The Direct Mail Sales Bureau plc
14 Floral Street
Covent Garden
London WC2E 9RR
01-379 7531

British List Brokers Association Ltd
Nassau House
122 Shaftesbury Avenue
London W1V 7DJ
01-734 4606

The Direct Mail Producers' Association
34 Grand Avenue
London N10 3BP
01-883 7229/444 4891

The Mail Users' Association Ltd
Communications House
137 Dulwich Road
London SE24 0NG
01-737 2425

The Direct Mail Services
Standards Board
92 New Cavendish Street
London W1M 7FA
01-636 7581

The Mail Order Traders'
Association
25 Castle Street
Liverpool L2 4TD
051-236 7581

Post Office Services
Post Office Direct Mail Section
Room 195
FREEPOST
33 Grosvenor Place
London SW1X 1EE

Chapter 8: Making News

KOGAN PAGE TITLE
Practical Sponsorship, Stuart Turner, 1987

USEFUL INFORMATION
The Writers' and Artists' Year Book, annual, A & C Black. Lists all publications, gives information on writing for radio, TV etc
Yellow Pages, for names of photographers

The Sponsorships Association
32 Sekforde Street
London EC1R 0HH
01-251 2505

Chapter 9: News Release Service

KOGAN PAGE TITLE
Practical Sponsorship, Stuart Turner, 1987

USEFUL INFORMATION
The Writers' and Artists' Year Book, annual, A & C Black, has a complete chapter on libel

Appendices 179

Chapter 11: Media Planning

REFERENCES
Advanti Advertising and Marketing, unpublished notes
Ray Morgan and Partners, *1987 Media Guide*

USEFUL INFORMATION
British Rate and Data (BRAD) for press information
1987 Media Guide, Ray Morgan and Partners
Yellow Pages

Audit Bureau of Circulation Ltd
13 Wimpole Street
London W1
01-631 1343
The ABC provides audited figures of circulation for most publications

PUBLICATIONS
Admap
Media Week
Media World

Chapter 12: Selecting an Advertising Agency

REFERENCES
Choosing and Using an Advertising Agency: The Directors' Guide, The Director Publications, 1985

KOGAN PAGE TITLE
London Creative Listings, 1987

USEFUL INFORMATION
Campaign Portfolio, Campaign Publications
12-14 Ansell Street
London W8
a list of advertising agencies

Selection services
The Advertising Agency Register
62 Shaftesbury Avenue
London W1V 7DE
Yellow Pages, for advertising agencies in your area

Chapter 13: Choosing a PR Consultancy

REFERENCES
Choosing and Using a PR Consultancy: The Director's Guide, The Director Publications, 1985

USEFUL INFORMATION
Public Relations Year Book, Public Relations Consultants Association/Financial Times. The official year book of PRCA lists member companies plus a lot of other useful information.
Yellow Pages will list local PR and publicity consultants

The Incorporated Society of British Advertisers
44 Hertford Street
London W1Y 8AE
01-499 7502

The Institute of Public Relations
Gate House
St John's Square
London EC1M 4DH
01-253 5151

The Public Relations Consultants Association
10 Belgrave Square
London SW1X 8PH
01-245 6444

The Public Relations Register
62 Shaftesbury Avenue
London W1V 7DE
01-437 3357

Useful addresses for general help and advice

Association of Independent Businesses
Trowbray House
108 Weston Street
London SE1 3QB
01-403 4066

Barclays Bank plc
Small Business Unit
54 Lombard Street
London EC3P 3AH
01-283 2161

British Exhibition Venues Association
36 Dudley Road
Royal Tunbridge Wells
Kent TN1 1LB

British Institute of Management
Management House
Cottingham Road
Corby
Northants NN17 1TT
0536 204222

British Overseas Trade Board
1-19 Victoria Street
London SW1H 0ET
01-215 7877

Business Statistics Office
Government Building
Cardiff Road
Newport
Gwent HP1 1XG
0633 5611

Central Office of Information
Hercules Road
London SE1 7DU
01-928 2345

Confederation of British Industry (CBI)
Centre Point
103 New Oxford Street
London WC1A 1DU
01-379 7400

Confederation of Irish Industry
Confederation House
Kildare Street
Dublin 2
0001 779801

Council for Small Industries in Rural Areas (CoSIRA)
141 Castle Street
Salisbury
Wilts SP1 3TP
0722 336255

Department of Employment
Small Firms and Tourism Division
Steel House
Tothill Street
London SW1H 9NF
01-213 3000

Small Firms Service
Phone Operator on 100 and ask for Freefone Enterprise to be put in touch with your nearest branch

North East
Centro House
3 Cloth Street
Newcastle upon Tyne NE1 3EE

North West
320-325 Royal Exchange Buildings
St Ann's Square
Manchester M2 7AH

Merseyside
Graeme House
Derby Square
Liverpool L3 9HJ

East Midlands
Severns House
20 Middle Pavement
Nottingham NG1 7DW

South East
Ebury House
2-18 Ebury Bridge Road
London SW1W 8QD
Tel 01-730 9678

South West
Fifth Floor
The Pithay
Bristol BS1 2NB

West
Abbey Hall
Abbey Square
Reading RG1 3BE

West Midlands
Sixth Floor
Ladywood House
Stephenson Street
Birmingham B2 4DT

Yorkshire and Humberside
1 Park Row
Leeds LS1 5NR

Development Board for Rural Wales
Ladywell House
Park Street
Newtown
Powys SY16 1JD
0686 26965

European Communities Commission
Press and Information Office
8 Storey's Gate
London SW1P 3AT
01-222 8122

The Forum of Private Business Ltd
Drury Lane
Knutsford
Cheshire WA16 6HA
0565 4467

Greater London Enterprise Board (GLEB)
Spencer House
63 Newington Causeway
London SE1 6BD
01-403 0300

Highlands and Islands Development Board
Bridge House
Bank Street
Inverness IV1 1QR
0463 234171

The Institute of Directors
116 Pall Mall
London SW1V 5ED
01-839 1233

Investors in Industry (3i)
91 Waterloo Road
London SE1 8XP
01-928 7822

Lloyds Bank plc
Small Business Unit
Monument Building
11-15 Monument Street
London EC3R 8JU
01-626 1500

The Local Enterprise Development Unit
Lamont House
Purdys Lane
Newtownbreda
Belfast BT8 4AR
0232 691031

Appendices 185

London Enterprise Agency
4 Snow Hill
London EC1A 2BS
01-236 3000

Midlands Bank plc
Small Business Unit
Customers should refer to their
local branch

The National Federation of Self Employed and
Small Businesses Ltd
32 St Annes Road (West)
Lytham St Annes
Lancs FY8 1NY

National Westminster Bank plc
Small Business Unit
3rd Floor
116 Fenchurch Street
London EC4
01-726 1000

Scottish Development Agency
   120 Boswell Street
   Glasgow G2 7JP
   041-248 2700

   102 Telford Road
   Edinburgh EH4 2NP
   031-343 1911

Trustee Savings Bank
3 Copthall Avenue
London EC2
01-588 9292

SPECIALIST LIBRARIES
British Institute of Management Library
Management House
Cottingham Road
Corby
Northants NN17 ITT
0536 20422

British Library Business Information Service
Science Reference Library
25 Southampton Buildings
Chancery Lane
London WC2A 1AW
01-404 0406

City University Business School Library
23 Goswell Road
London EC1M 7BB
01-253 4399 ext 573

London Business School Library
Sussex Place
Regent's Park
London NW1 4SA
01-262 5050

Index

Activities, special 96
adoption stages 14
advertisement design
   facilities 55
advertisements:
   measuring the 154
   producing professional 56
   without illustrations 60
advertising 12-22, 173; *see also*
   press advertisements
   burst 151
   codes of practice 20-22
   continuous 151
   costs of 20
   direct response 12, 77-94, 177
   dishonesty in 13
   economics of 145-6
   frequency of 18-19
   indirect response 12
   misconceptions about 12-13
   rules for effective 16-20
   timing of 19-20
   types of 13-14
   weight of 147-56
advertising agency 55, 144
   paying the 161
   selecting an 157-61, 179-80
Advertising Agency
   Register 159, 180
Advertising Association 21-2, 174
advertising campaign:
   creative execution of 49-50
   creative strategy 46
   determining weight of 148-56
advertising features 60-61
Advertising Standards
   Authority 21, 174
advertorial packages 155-6
advertorials 60-61
allocation of money to
   promotion 125-6
artist, commercial 55
artwork:
   care of 58
   checking the 56-8
   stages of producing 58
Associated Newspapers
   Group Ltd 90
Association of Mail Order
   Publishers 22, 174

Blocks 58
brand names 10
British Code of Advertising 21
British Code of Sales Promotion
   Practice 21
British Rate and Data
   (BRAD) 138, 146
budgeting 171
budgets, setting 127-8
Bulk Rebates Service 94
business:
   defining your 3-5

promoting your own 1-11
Business Reply paid cards and envelopes 94
business to users advertising 13

Cancellation of advertisements 156
cash flow 171
catalogues 79-84
   advantages 81
   benefits to the customer 81-2
   presentation 81
   risks and dangers of 82
   successful 82-4
CEEFAX 132
Churchill, David 25
cinema 139-40
classified advertisements 59-60
cocktail parties 33
Code of Advertising Practice Committee 21
codes of practice, advertising 20-22
coding advertisements 153
commercial artist 55
Communication, Advertising and Marketing Education Foundation Ltd (CAM) 22, 174
company name 9
competitions 28, 31-2
conferences 33, 96
consumer advertising 13
consumers 25
copy:
   direct mail letter 73-4
   writing 50-55
cost of advertising 20
cost-effectiveness of PR 26
costing 171
coupons 28
credit cards 88
cross-selling 84
customer protection 88-94
customer service 10-11
customers, and potential customers 7
cut-off points 129

Daily Telegraph Ltd, The 90
'Dealers Protection Scheme' 89
defining your business 3
design, of press advertisement 50, 176-7
designer:
   briefing the 56
   selecting a 55-6
designing leaflets 66-73
designing posters 61-6
direct mail 141, 147
   letters 73-6
Direct Mail Deposit System 94
direct mailing, errors 73
direct marketing, *see* direct response advertising
direct response advertising 77-94, 177
   principles of 78
   success in 77-8
   supporting the campaign 88
direct response market sequence 78-9
directories 143
discounts, special 28
discounts in advertising 155
display space, choice of position 154
ditribution channels 7-8
door-to-door deliveries 85

Early users 14
employees 8, 26; *see also* staff
events 33-4
Exhibition Bulletin 41
exhibitions 41-4, 175
   staff behaviour at 42-3
   tips for 41-2
experience records 18
Express Newspapers Ltd 90

Feature articles 101-2
financial planning, of

Index

promotional activity 124-9
Financial Times Ltd 90
First Class Letter Contracts 94
free samples 28
Freepost 94
funds, for advertising, finding 20

Giveaways 143
guarantees 85
Guardian & Manchester Evening News Ltd, The 90

Headline 51-2
hired photographer 123
hospitality tents and rooms 33-4
'house style' 9
Household Delivery Service 94

IBM Action Writer 74
illustration:
  poster 64
  for press advertisement 50
image 2-5, 171
  assessing your 4
  packaging your 9-11
  product 35
  reinforcing your 10-11
Incentive Discounts for Growth 94
income levels in target audience 17-18
Incorporated Society of British Advisers 89, 174
information, further in press advertisement 53-4
inserts, into magazines 85
Institute of Practitioners in Advertising 89
Institute of Public Relations 24, 175
interest groups, for targeting PR 25-6
intermediaries 7-8
interview:
  radio 107
  television 106
Introductory Offer, Royal Mail 94

Journalists 8

Kelly's trade directory 7

Law, on product information 36
lead time 154-5
leaflet holder 68
leaflets 66-73, 142
  care of 72
  checking quantities 72
  costs 71
  designing 66-73
  duplicating 73
  holder for 68
  printing 72-3
  suitable for the task intended 67-71
letters:
  direct mail 73-6
  duplicate 74
  individually typed 74
  printed 74
local business, media for the 141
local community 8, 25
local press 147
  visits 97-8
logos 10
  use of, in mail order 93

Magazines 135
  insertions into 85
  readership profile 136-7
mail discounts and services for direct mail advertisers 94
mail order 22, 88-94
  schemes for customer protection 88-94
Mail Order Protection Scheme (MOPS) 89-93
mailing lists 73
  ways to obtain 84-5

market, checklist of data
  for your 6
Marketing Week 86-7
media 130
  and PR 23
media independents 144-5
media plan, making a 144-7
media planning 130-56, 179
media schedule 156
merchandising, in-store
  34-6, 175
message:
  competitive and
    stimulating 16-17
  targeting 17-18
middlemen, conflict with 78
Mirror Group Newspapers
  Ltd 90
MOPS (Mail Order Protection
  Scheme) 89-93
  application for
    membership 91
  exemptions from 92-3
  fees 92
  use of logos 93

Name, company 9
National Newspaper Association
  Ltd 89-90
National Newspapers Mail Order
Protection Scheme Ltd, add 91
news:
  making 95-107, 178
  targeting 25-6
News Group Newspapers
  Ltd 90
news release:
  presentation and
    despatching 115-21
  writing a 108-15
news release service 108-23,
  178-9
news stories 95-8
Newspaper Publishers'
  Association 89
Newspaper Publishing Plc 90

Newspaper Society, The 89
newspapers:
  local evening 135
  local weekly 138
  national 133-4
  readership profile 134
  regional daily 135

Observer Ltd, The 90
offers:
  special 29-30
  trial 31
Office of Fair Trading 89
open days 33
opinion formers 8, 25
ORACLE 132-3
organisation image 171
'overs and unders' 72
Oxfam 65

Packaging, product 34-7
payback calculations 126-7
Periodical Publishers'
  Association Ltd 89
periodicals, readership
  profile 136
personal selling, benefits of 39
personality stories 96-7
photographers 122-3
photographs 119-21
  personal 107
  sending out 121
pictures, sending out 121
planning:
  financial 124-9
  media 130-156
  promotional activities
    165-71
point-of-sale (POS) 34, 36
  material 36
Post Office services 84-5, 94,
  178
postcards 141
posters 140-41, 147
  designing 62-6
  hand-produced 64-6

Index

limitations of 66
PR consultancy, choosing a 162-4, 180
PR (Public Relations):
  activities 26-7
  cost-effectiveness 26
  definition of 24
  evaluating 27
  further information 174-5
  role of 24
presentation of a news release 115-21
press 133-8
press advertisements:
  designing 45-61, 176-7
  other types 59-61
press information 146-7
press photographer 122-3
press receptions 98-100
press visits, local 97-8
price-offs 28
pricing 171
product:
  packaging 34-7
  position in market 48
  unique feature 46-8
product adoption, stages in 14-15
product image 35
product maker's mindest 47
product news 95-6
projecting the organisation 97-101
promoting your own business 1-11, 173
promotion, successful, keys to 5-9
promotional activities, planning your 165-71
promotional activity, financial planning of 124-9
promotional news 95-6
promotional tools 1-2
protection of customer, in mail order schemes 88-94

public relations (PR) 23-7
public speaking 143
publicity:
  gaining countrywide 100-101
  national 101-4
  regional 100-101
Radio 102-4, 107, 139
records, to define potential customers 18
regional publicity 100-101
reporters 121-2
reputation 2-5
research, desk 18
response patterns to advertising 151-2
retailers 25
Royal Mail, services and discounts to direct mail advertisers 94; *and see* Post Office services

Sales campaign, success of 85-8
sales and marketing 171
sales promotion 28-34, 175
  activities 28-9
  types of 29-34
sales training 38
Scottish Daily Newspaper Society 89
Scottish Newspaper Proprietors' Association 89
Second Class Discount 94
selling 38-40, 175
  personal, benefits of 39
semi-display advertisements 60
service:
  follow-up 88
  unique feature 46-8
shareholders 25
shop window displays 142
skills, managing your own and those of your staff 171-2

space, buying advertising 153-4
special offers 29-30
sponsorship 32-3, 97, 178
sports activities 97
staff 8
    behaviour at exhibitions 42-3
staff outings 96
Stamping, Methods of 94
stationery 9
stunts 34
style of copy 54-5
successful business, ingredients for 2-3
successful promotion, keys to 5-9
suppliers 8

Tack, Alfred, *How to Overcome Nervous Tension and Speak Well in Public* 143
target audience 6-9
    groups 17-18
    for press advertisements 48-9
targeting news 25-6
targets, sales 38-9
telemarketing 39-40, 87

telephone selling 39-40
teletext 132
television 102-6, 130-33
    appearing on 104-6
Thomson Local 143
Times Newspapers Ltd 90
timing of advertising 19-20
tools, promotional 1-2
'trade', the 7-8
trade advertising 13
Trade Descriptions Act 93
trade marks 10
trade services 101
training:
    sales 38
    in telephone selling 40
trial offers 31
Tunstall Lifeline 68-70

Unique selling point (USP) 46-8
useful addresses 181-2
users, early, influence on the market 15-16

wholesalers 25
words, for press advertisement 50

Yellow Pages 19, 84, 143